Practical Rust Projects

Building Game, Physical Computing, and Machine Learning Applications

Shing Lyu

Apress®

Practical Rust Projects: Building Game, Physical Computing, and Machine Learning Applications

Shing Lyu
Amsterdam, The Netherlands

ISBN-13 (pbk): 978-1-4842-5598-8   ISBN-13 (electronic): 978-1-4842-5599-5
https://doi.org/10.1007/978-1-4842-5599-5

Managing Director, Apress Media LLC: Welmoed Spahr
Acquisitions Editor: Steve Anglin
Development Editor: Matthew Moodie
Editorial Operations Manager: Mark Powers

Cover designed by eStudioCalamar

Cover image designed by Freepik (www.freepik.com)

Distributed to the book trade worldwide by Apress Media, LLC, 1 New York Plaza, New York, NY 10004, U.S.A. Phone 1-800-SPRINGER, fax (201) 348-4505, e-mail orders-ny@springer-sbm.com, or visit www.springeronline.com. Apress Media, LLC is a California LLC and the sole member (owner) is Springer Science + Business Media Finance Inc (SSBM Finance Inc). SSBM Finance Inc is a **Delaware** corporation.

For information on translations, please e-mail editorial@apress.com; for reprint, paperback, or audio rights, please email bookpermissions@springernature.com.

Apress titles may be purchased in bulk for academic, corporate, or promotional use. eBook versions and licenses are also available for most titles. For more information, reference our Print and eBook Bulk Sales web page at http://www.apress.com/bulk-sales.

Any source code or other supplementary material referenced by the author in this book is available to readers on GitHub via the book's product page, located at www.apress.com/9781484255988. For more detailed information, please visit http://www.apress.com/source-code.

Printed on acid-free paper

*For my wife Wei-Chi, my father Ching-Chuan,
and my mother Man-Yun.*

Table of Contents

About the Author xi

About the Technical Reviewer xiii

Chapter 1: Welcome to the World of Rust 1

Who Is This Book For?..2

Who Is This Book *Not* For? 3

Criteria for Selecting Libraries 4

    Pure Rust..4

    Maturity 5

    Popularity 5

How To Use This Book 6

    Chapter Overview 6

Source Code...7

Chapter 2: Building a Command-Line Program 9

Introduction..9

What Are You Building? 10

Creating a Binary Project 11

Reading Command-Line Arguments with std::env::args....................12

Handling Complex Arguments with StructOpt...............................14

Adding Binary Flags (aka Switches) 18

Printing to STDERR...19

Printing with Color 21

Reading the Cat Picture from a File 22

Better Error Handling 26

Piping to Other Commands 31

    Piping to STDOUT Without Color 32

    Accepting STDIN 33

Integration Testing 34

Publishing and Distributing the Program 39

    Install from Source 39

    Publish to crates.io 40

    Building Binaries for Distribution 41

Conclusion 42

Chapter 3: Creating Graphical User Interfaces (GUIs) 43

What Are You Building? 44

Building a Text-Based User Interface 46

Showing a Dialog Box 48

Handling Simple Keyboard Inputs 50

Adding a Dialog 51

Multi-Step Dialogs 53

Reading User Input 56

Moving to Graphical User Interfaces (GUIs) 59

Creating a Window 60

Displaying an Image 63

Using Glade to Design the UI 66

Accepting Inputs and Button Clicks 77

Reading a gtk::Switch 82

Other Alternatives 85

Chapter 4: Building a Game 87

What Are You Building? 87

Amethyst and the Entity-Component-System Pattern 88

Creating an Amethyst Project..90

Creating a Window 92

Seeing the World Through a Camera.....................................97

Adding the Cats...100

Moving the Cats 109

Creating the Ball 117

Can't Defy Gravity 121

Making the Ball Bounce 125

Keeping Score...132

Let There Be Music 142

Other Alternatives 153

Chapter 5: Physical Computing in Rust 155

What Are You Building? 156

Physical Computing on Raspberry Pi...................................157

Getting to Know Your Raspberry Pi....................................157

Install Raspbian Through NOOBS.......................................158

Install the Rust Toolchain...160

Controlling the GPIO Pins..161

Building a LED Circuit 163

Controlling the GPIO Output from Rust 166

Reading Button Clicks 170

Cross-Compiling to Raspberry Pi 177

How Does the GPIO Code Work? 179

Where Do You Go from Here? 184

Chapter 6: Artificial Intelligence and Machine Learning 187

What Is Machine Learning? 187

    Supervised vs. Unsupervised Learning 188

What Are You Building? 189

Introducing the rusty-machine Crate 191

Clustering Cat Breeds with K-Means 193

    Introduction to the K-Means Algorithm 193

    The Training Data 195

    Exporting as CSV 200

    Moving the Configuration Into a File 202

    Visualizing the Data 207

    Setting Up K-Means 211

Detecting Cats versus Dogs with the Neural Network 218

    Introduction to Neural Networks 218

    Preparing the Training and Testing Data 221

    Setting Up the Neural Network Model 224

    Reading the Training and Testing Data 224

    Normalizing the Training Data 227

    Training and Predicting 230

    Making the Prediction 232

Other Alternatives 234

Chapter 7: What Else Can You Do with Rust? 237

The End Is Just the Beginning 237

The Web 237

Backend..238

Frontend 241

Web Browser and Crawler..242

Mobile...244

Operating Systems and Embedded Devices..............................248

Unlimited Possibilities of Rust..249

Index...251

About the Author

 **Shing Lyu** has worked professionally on one of the biggest Rust projects, the Firefox's Gecko engine, as well as on its upstream project, the Servo browser engine. He is the co-creator of RustPython, which has over 4.7k stars on GitHub. Shing was also active in building the local Rust community in Taiwan.

Besides Rust, Shing writes about all sorts of programming topics on his blog at `https://shinglyu.com`. He has also authored video courses, given talks at conferences, and mentored other open source contributors. Shing has worked for many companies, including Mozilla, Booking.com, Intel, and DAZN.

About the Technical Reviewer

 **Michael Sawyer** is a lead security engineer working in the San Francisco Bay area. A native to Northern California, Michael attended CSU, Chico, where he earned a BS in Computer Science with a minor in Mathematics. With more than five years in the industry, Michael enjoys tinkering with all ranges of computational devices, from Kubernetes in the cloud, to embedded systems and field-programmable gate arrays. Visit his website at `https://michaelasawyer.com/`.

CHAPTER 1

Welcome to the World of Rust

If you are reading this book, you are probably as excited about Rust as I am. Since its first stable release in 2015, Rust has come a long way in terms of features and stability. Developers around the world are fascinated about how Rust can combine features that were once thought as unavoidable tradeoffs: performance with memory safety and low-level control with productivity. Despite the infamous steep learning curve, Rust has gained popularity over the years. It was named the "most loved programming language" in the StackOverflow survey four years in a row, from 2016 to 2019. Many big companies and organizations, including Facebook, Microsoft, Dropbox, and npm, have started using Rust in production.

What are people using Rust for? If you take a look at `crates.io`, the official Rust crates (libraries) registry, there are over 28,900 crates and over a billion downloads. There are 47 categories on `crates.io`[1], ranging from command-line interfaces, cryptography, databases, games, operating systems, web programming, and many more. What does it feel like to use these libraries? How does Rust's syntax and design philosophy affect the design of these crates? This book will try to answer these questions.

---

[1]`https://crates.io/categories`

© Shing Lyu 2020
S. Lyu, *Practical Rust Projects*, https://doi.org/10.1007/978-1-4842-5599-5_1

Who Is This Book For?

This book will be useful for:

- People who already know basic Rust syntax, but want to learn how to build applications in Rust.

- People who are considering using Rust to build production-ready systems.

- People who want a quick overview of high-level architecture and programming interface design in other fields.

You might have learned about Rust out of curiosity. After finishing all the tutorials and beginner books, you might be wondering, "What should I do next? What can I build with Rust?" This book will walk you through a few different applications of Rust, which will help you move beyond theories and into building real applications. Rust has a fascinating design and many interesting language features, but simply knowing how to write basic algorithms and data structures won't necessarily prepare you for building useful applications. I tried to find the most production-ready but also modern Rust libraries to do the job, so you'll be able to judge if Rust is ready for the application you have envisioned. If it's not, you might even find opportunities to contribute to Rust's community by improving the existing libraries, frameworks, and design or by building new ones.

You might have used Rust for a specific project—maybe a CLI tool for work or an open-source browser engine that happens to use Rust. Once you master Rust for that domain, it's beneficial to learn Rust for other domains, say when building a game or website. This will bring you unexpected ideas. For example, by building a game, you can learn how game engine designers organize their code to make it decoupled and easy to maintain. You may never build a game for work, but that architectural knowledge might influence the architecture of your next project.

Another example is that learning how cross-compiling to a Raspberry Pi might help you understand how compiling to WebAssembly works. So this book is aimed to take you through a tour of various applications of Rust. You'll learn how their application programming interfaces (APIs)[2] look and how they organize their code and architecture.

Who Is This Book *Not* For?

This book might not be that useful for:

- People who want to learn the Rust programming language itself.

- People who want to dive deep into one particular field.

- People who are looking for the most experimental and cutting-edge Rust implementations.

This book is not a course on the Rust programming language itself, nor is it trying to teach Rust's syntax via examples. It focuses on the applications themselves and their domain knowledge, assuming you already know Rust's syntax and language features. There are many excellent books on Rust itself, like *The Rust Programming Language* by Steve Klabnik and Carol Nichols. You can also find online books, interactive tutorials, and videos on the "Learn Rust" section of the official website[3]. Each of the topics in this book can easily be expanded into a book of its own, so I try to give you a high-level understanding of the topic, but won't go too deep into them. I aim to give you a broad overview of what is possible with Rust and what the developer experience is like. Therefore, the examples are simplified so people without a background

---

[2]I use the term API in a general sense. This includes the functions, structs, and command-line tools exposed by each library or framework.

[3]https://www.rust-lang.org/learn

in that particular field can still get a taste of the mental model of the field. Also, I'm not advocating that the methods presented in the book are the "best" or most trendy way of building those applications. I tried to strike a balance between being modern and being pragmatic.

Criteria for Selecting Libraries

Rust is a relatively young language. Therefore it's a big challenge to select the libraries or frameworks to use in each chapter. On the one end, there are experimental pure-Rust implementations for almost every field. Many proof-of-concept libraries compete with each other without a clear winner. The early adopters of Rust are usually adventurous developers; they are comfortable with rough edges in the libraries and find workarounds. The focus is on experimentation, learning, and innovation, but not necessarily on user-friendliness. On the other end, people are seeking stability and production-readiness. Because of Rust's great interoperability with other programming languages, there are many attempts to write a Rust wrapper around mature C/C++ (or other languages) libraries. In this book, I demonstrate the core concept in each field and what its Rust API design looks like. Therefore, when selecting the libraries for each chapter, I used the following criteria.

Pure Rust

I try to find libraries that are built purely in Rust. Rust's FFI (foreign function interface) allows you to call existing C libraries (and many other languages) from Rust. Therefore, the easiest way to build Rust applications quickly is to leverage existing libraries in other languages. These libraries are usually designed with other languages in mind, so wrapping them in Rust results in a weird and not idiomatic Rust API. When there is a pure Rust library or a library using existing technology but built from scratch using Rust, I tend to choose those.

Maturity

Not every pure Rust library is mature. Because many Rust libraries are built from a clean slate, developers often try to use the latest experimental technology, but that might mean that the architecture and API design are very experimental and change frequently. Some of these libraries showed great potential in their early days, but then the development slowed down, and the projects went into maintenance mode or were even abandoned. This book aims to build useful software rather than experiment with exciting technologies and throw the code away. Therefore, I preferred to be pragmatic and choose a library that is mature enough and uses widely-accepted design patterns, rather than be dogmatic about using pure-Rust libraries. I choose to use a GTK+-based library in Chapter 3 for this reason.

Popularity

If two or more library candidates meet the previous criteria (are pure Rust and are mature), I choose the most popular one. The popularity is based on a combination of factors:

- Number of downloads on `crates.io`

- Pace of development and release

- Discussions on issue trackers and discussion forums

- Media coverage

Although popularity is not a guarantee of success, a popular project is more likely to have a large community the supports it and keeps it alive. This can help you find a library that has the most potential to stick around in the future. You are also more likely to get support and answers online.

How To Use This Book

The chapters in this book are independent of each other, so you can read them in any order you want. However, some of the ideas and design patterns are used in multiple chapters. I try to introduce these ideas in the chapter where the design originated, or where it makes the most sense. For example, the concept of using event handlers to build a responsive user interface is introduced in the text-based user interface section in Chapter 3, and then referenced in Chapter 4. So reading the book sequentially might help you build this knowledge in an incremental way.

Chapter Overview

Chapter 2 starts with the easiest application you can build with Rust: a command-line interface (CLI). Building a CLI requires very minimal setup and background knowledge, but can produce very powerful applications. I introduce how to read raw arguments using the standard library, then I show you how to use StructOpt to manage arguments better and create features like generating a help message for free. I also touch upon topics like piping, testing, and publishing the program to crates.io.

Chapter 3 shows you how to build two-dimensional interfaces. You'll first build a text-based 2D interface using the Cursive text-based user interface system. This allows you to build interactive user interfaces like popups, buttons, and forms. The experience in the text-based user interface (TUI) paved the way for a graphical user interface (GUI). I'll be introducing the Rust binding for the popular GTK+ 3 library, gtk-rs. You'll build the same interactive form using the GUI library.

In Chapter 4, you'll be building a game in Rust. You'll use the Amethyst game engine to make a cat volleyball game. You'll learn the design philosophy behind Amethyst, which is called the Entity-Component-System. You'll learn how to create 2D games, rendering the characters and items with a spritesheet. You'll also implement game logic like collision detection, keeping score, and adding sound effects and background music.

In Chapter 5, you'll connect the virtual world with the physical world. I introduce physical computing on a Raspberry Pi development board. You'll start by installing a full operating system and install the whole Rust toolchain on the device, and you'll learn how to use Rust to control an LED and how to take inputs from a physical button. Then I show you how to cross-compile Rust on another computer to produce a binary that runs on a Raspberry Pi.

In Chapter 6, the focus shifts to artificial intelligence and machine learning. I show you how to implement an unsupervised and supervised machine learning model using the `rusty-machine` crate. For the unsupervised model, I introduce K-means, and for the supervised model, I demonstrate the neural network. I also show you how to do some data processing tasks like test data generation, reading/writing CSV files, and visualization.

Finally, Chapter 7 contains a broad overview of other exciting fields in Rust that didn't make it into the other chapters. I point you to cool projects in areas like operating systems, web browsers, web servers backend, serverless applications, and frontend (WebAssembly). This final chapter can act as a guidebook for your future exploration into the vast world of Rust.

Source Code

All the source code for this book is available on GitHub: `https://www.github.com/apress/practical-rust-projects`. The source code is also accessible via the Download Source Code button located at `www.apress.com/9781484255988`.

When I include source code in the book, I highlight the part that is relevant to the point being discussed. The non-relevant part is omitted with a comment like this:

```
// ...
```

Therefore, not all code examples in the book can be compiled successfully. To see the full working example, check the source code on GitHub.

Most of the examples are developed and tested on a Linux (Ubuntu 16.04) machine. The Rust version is `stable-x86_64-unknown-unchanged` - `rustc 1.39.0 (4560ea788 2019-11-04)`. The stable version is used as much as possible, but certain libraries require use of the nightly version.

CHAPTER 2

Building a Command-Line Program

Introduction

Command-line programs, also known as CLIs (command-line interfaces), are one of the most natural applications of Rust. When you compile your first Hello World program, you are building a command-line program. A typical command-line program takes arguments, flags, and sometimes standard input and then executes its main algorithm and output to the standard output or file. All these operations are well supported by the Rust standard library and the third-party crates on `crates.io`.

There are a few advantages to building a CLI in Rust. First, the rich collection of libraries on `crates.io` will enable you to achieve many things you need. Second, its high performance and safety guarantees let you mitigate many performance bottlenecks and bugs, compared to other popular scripting languages like Python or Ruby. Finally, Rust programs can be compiled into a single, small binary containing platform-specific machine code for easy distribution, so users don't need to have a language runtime on their systems.

One example of this space is the `ripgrep`[1] project. It is a line-oriented search tool like GNU grep, ack, or The Silver Searcher. Ripgrep has exceptional performance. It outperforms C-based GNU grep in many

---

[1]`https://github.com/BurntSushi/ripgrep`

© Shing Lyu 2020
S. Lyu, *Practical Rust Projects*, https://doi.org/10.1007/978-1-4842-5599-5_2

benchmarks[2]. But at the same time, it doesn't need to reinvent every wheel. Ripgrep builds on top of many existing libraries, like the regex crate (regular expression parsing, compiling, and execution) and the clap crate (command-line argument parsing). This is a perfect example of how Rust can be fast and easy to write at the same time.

What Are You Building?

Cowsay is a funny little command-line program originally written in Perl. It takes a text message and renders an ASCII-art cow (it looks more like a horse to me, to be honest) saying that message in a speech bubble (see Figure 2-1). Although this program seems pretty useless, it's still quite popular on UNIX servers, where the system administrator can use it to print a light-hearted welcome message to the user.

Cowsay has a very simple algorithm, so by using it as an example, I can focus on the mechanisms and tooling to build a command-line program, instead of focusing on the business logic. We all know that cats are the unofficial mascot of the Internet, so you are going to build a catsay tool that makes a cat speak your message. The features include:

- Take a string as the positional argument.

- Take a -d/--dead flag that makes the cat's eyes become xx, which is the comical expression of dead eyes.

- Take a -h/--help flag to print a help message.

- Take a -v/--version flag to print the version information.

- Print the image in color.

- Error handling: print any error message to STDERR.

---

[2]https://blog.burntsushi.net/ripgrep/

- Piping: accept STDIN as input and allow the output to be piped to other programs.

- Run integration tests.

- Package and publish the tool to crates.io.

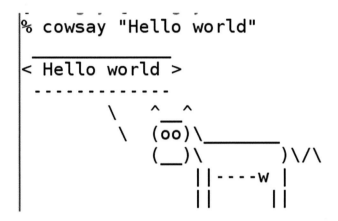

Figure 2-1. *Example output of cowsay*

Creating a Binary Project

Although you can simply write an .rs file and compile it with rustc, handling dependencies will be a nightmare. Therefore, you are going to use *Cargo*, Rust's package manager, to create a project and handle the dependencies for you. Cargo is capable of creating two kinds of projects—binaries and libraries. *Libraries* are used to build packages that are intended to be used as building blocks for other programs. *Binaries* are what you are trying to build in this chapter: single programs that are used independently. To create a binary program, run the following command in your terminal:

```
$ cargo new --bin catsay
    Created binary (application) 'catsay' package
```

The --bin flag stands for "binary," which tells Cargo to create the package as a binary program. You can also omit the flag because it's the default.

The command creates a catsay folder and some basic files, as shown in Listing 2-1.

Listing 2-1. Folder Structure and Files Created by Cargo

```
catsay
|-- Cargo.toml
+-- src
    +-- main.rs
```

If you open main.rs, there will be a Hello World program template already created for you. To run the Hello World example, simply run this in the terminal inside the catsay folder:

```
$ cargo run
```

This will compile your project and execute the code in your main.rs file. (To be more precise, run the fn main() function in your main.rs.)

Reading Command-Line Arguments with std::env::args

The first thing you'll implement is the process of showing the text passed as a string in the cat's speech bubble:

```
$ cargo run -- "Hello I'm a cat"
   Compiling catsay v0.1.0 (/path/to/catsay)
    Finished dev [unoptimized + debuginfo] target(s) in 1.18s
     Running 'target/debug/catsay 'Hello I'\"m a cat"
```

```
Hello I'm a cat
 \
  \
     /\_/\
    ( o o )
    =( I )=
```

Note   The -- following `cargo run` signifies the end of options (to `cargo`); all the arguments following the -- will be passed to the main program in `main.rs`, which is the compiled binary `target/debug/catsay`, as you can see from the `Running...` line in the output. Also, keep in mind that the `Compiling ...`, `Finished ...`, and `Running ...` lines are the logs from Cargo itself. The program's output starts after the `Running ...` line.

Printing the text and the cat is pretty straightforward with `println!()`, but how do you actually read the command-line argument? Thanks to the Rust standard library, you can use `std::env::args()`, as shown in Listing 2-2.

Listing 2-2. Reading an Argument with std::env::args

```rust
fn main() {
    let message = std::env::args().nth(1)
        .expect("Missing the message. Usage: catsay < message>");
    println!("{}", message);
    println!(" \\");
    println!("  \\");
    println!("     /\\_/\\");
    println!("    ( o o )");
    println!("    =( I )=");
}
```

The `std::env::args()` function returns an iterator to the arguments. The 0th argument is the name of the binary itself, `catsay`, and the string you are looking for is the next argument, so you can call the `nth(1)` function on the iterator to get the first argument. The `nth()` function might fail (e.g., if n is larger than the size of the iterator) and return an `Option::None`, so you can use `unwrap` or `expect` to get the contained value. Then you assign this value to a variable named `message` and print it out using `println!()`.

Handling Complex Arguments with StructOpt

The `std::env::args` function works well for small programs with only a few options. But once you have more and more options, it becomes cumbersome to parse them by hand. For example, you might have flags that have a long and short version, e.g., `--version` and `-v`. Or you might have optional arguments that take values (e.g., `--option value`). These types of arguments are prevalent in command-line tools, but implementing them from scratch every time is a real pain. One solution to this is to use the `clap` library[3]. `Clap` can help you generate a parser for the arguments. You just have to declare the arguments you need in Rust code or YAML, then `clap` generates the command-line parser and a nice-looking `--help` message for you.

To make your life even simpler, there is the great library called `StructOpt`[4] that combines `clap` and custom derive. Custom derive is a feature in Rust that automatically generates a default implementation of a trait by annotating a struct. You can define a struct containing the arguments you want and annotate it with `#[derive(StructOpt)]`. A macro defined by

---

[3]Clap stands for Command-Line Argument Parser; see `https://clap.rs/`
[4]`https://crates.io/crates/structopt`

the StructOpt automatically implements the StructOpt trait for the struct. This implementation will contain the necessary clap code for parsing the arguments. You can get the parsed arguments in the struct format you defined. It's much more declarative, and the parsed struct is very easy to manipulate. To use StructOpt to parse your string input, you first need to add it to the [dependencies] section in the Cargo.toml file:

```
[package]
name = "catsay"
version = "0.1.0"
authors = ["Shing Lyu <my@email.com>"]
edition = "2018"

[dependencies]
structopt = "0.2.15"
```

Then you can change the code, as shown in Listing 2-3.

Listing 2-3. Reading a Single Positional Argument Using StructOpt

```
extern crate structopt;

use structopt::StructOpt;

#[derive(StructOpt)]
struct Options {
    message: String // [1]
}

fn main() {
    let options = Options::from_args();   // [2]
    let message = options.message;
    println!("{}", message);
    // ... print the cat
}
```

In [1], you define a struct named Options that has one String field called message. Then you annotate the struct with the custom derive attribute #[derive(StructOpt)]. This way StructOpt will take the struct as the argument definition and generate the argument parsers accordingly. To actually parse the arguments in main(), you call Options::from args(), which parses the arguments and fills them into the Options struct and returns it. You can then access the individual fields like a normal Rust struct (e.g., options.message).

Let's see how that looks in action. One nice thing you get for free when using StructOpt is a --help command:

```
$ cargo run -- --help
    Finished dev [unoptimized + debuginfo] target(s) in 21.02s
     Running 'target/debug/catsay  --help'
catsay 0.1.0
Shing Lyu <my@email.com>

USAGE:
    catsay <message>

FLAGS:
    -h, --help          Prints help information
    -V, --version       Prints version information

ARGS:
    <message>
```

As you can see in the help message, you have a positional argument named <message>.

If you forget to provide the message argument, StructOpt is smart enough to show an error message:

```
$ cargo run
    Finished dev [unoptimized + debuginfo] target(s) in 0.04s
```

```
    Running 'target/debug/catsay'
error: The following required arguments were not provided:
    <message>

USAGE:
    catsay <message>

For more information try --help
```

However, in the current implementation, you only know there is an argument called message, but new users will not know what it is for. They also won't know what kind of value it should be. To improve the help message, you can include a description of that field and add a default value for it. If you don't provide the message argument, the default value will be used (see Listing 2-4).

Listing 2-4. Configuring the Default Value and Description

```
struct Options{
  #[structopt(default_value = "Meow!")]
  /// What does the cat say?
  message: String,
}
```

The field is annotated with #[structopt(default_value= "<default>")], which sets a default value for the field. The next line looks like a comment in Rust, but it starts with a triple / instead of double. These kinds of comments are documentation comments, which are normally used for Rust documentation (e.g., the rustdoc tools use it). StructOpt will pick that up and use it as the description for that field.

The help message will then become:

```
ARGS:
    <message>   What does the cat say?  [default: Meow!]
```

Adding Binary Flags (aka Switches)

StructOpt makes it really easy to add binary flags, also known as toggles or switches. Cowsay has a flag called --dead (-d), which will change the cow's eye from an "o" symbol to an "x," a classic, comical expression of death. You can easily implement this by adding the code to the Options struct, as shown in Listing 2-5.

Listing 2-5. Adding a Binary Flag Called --dead

```
#[derive(StructOpt)]
struct Options {
    message: String,

    #[structopt(short = "d",  long = "dead")]
    /// Make the cat appear dead
    dead: bool,
}
```

You add a field of type bool named dead. You can assign the long and short version of the flag by annotating the field with #[structopt(short = "d", long= "dead")]. The help message will now look like this:

```
FLAGS:
    -d, --dead        Makes the cat appear dead
    -h, --help         Prints help information
    -V, --version    Prints version information
```

To use the flag, you can modify the main() function, as shown in Listing 2-6.

Listing 2-6. Showing Different Eyes Based on the Options::dead Flag

```
let options = Options::from_args();
let message = options.message;

let eye = if options.dead { "x" } else { "o" }; // [1]

println!("{}", message);
println!(" \\");
println!("  \\");
println!("     /\\_/\\");
println!("    ( {eye} {eye} )", eye=eye); // [2]
println!("    =( I )=");
```

When a flag has the bool type, its values are determined by the presence of it. If the flag is not present, it will be set to false and vice versa. In [1], you assign the eye variable to o or x, based on whether options.dead is true or false. Then in [2], you use println!() and interpolate the {eye} part into the desired eye character.

There are other types of arguments called *options*, which can take a value (e.g., --value myvalue), and I cover them in the section entitled "Printing with Color". Let's shift the focus to how to handle output.

Printing to STDERR

Up until now, you have been printing using println!(), which prints to the standard output (STDOUT). However, there is also the standard error (STDERR) stream that you can and should print errors to. Rust provides a STDERR equivalent of println!(), called eprintln!(). The e- prefix stands for error. You can see this in action by printing an error when the user tries to make the cat say "woof" (see Listing 2-7).

Listing 2-7. Printing to STDERR When an Error Happens

```
fn main() {
    // ...
    if message.to_lowercase() == "woof" {
        eprintln!("A cat shouldn't bark like a dog.")
    }
    // ...
}
```

You can test this by redirecting the STDOUT and STDERR streams to separate files:

```
cargo run "woof" 1> stdout.txt 2> stderr.txt
```

The two files will look like Listing 2-8. An interesting fact is that cargo run actually prints its log (i.e., the Compiling..., Finished... message) to STDERR. If you want to print without a newline at the end of each line, you can use print!() and eprint!().

Listing 2-8. The Contents of stdout.txt and stderr.txt

```
$ cat stdout.txt
woof
 \
  \
      /\_/\
     ( o o )
     =( I )=
$ cat stderr.txt
   Compiling catsay v0.1.0 (/home/shinglyu/workspace/practical_
   rust/chap_1_cli/catsay)
    Finished dev [unoptimized + debuginfo] target(s) in 1.89s
     Running 'target/debug/catsay woof'
A cat shouldn't bark like a dog.
```

Printing with Color

Modern terminals (or terminal emulators) are usually capable of printing in color. In this section, you are going to make the catsay more colorful using the colored crate. First you need to add colored to the Cargo.toml file:

```
[dependencies]
// ...
colored = "1.7.0"
```

Then in the main.rs file, you need to extern the crate and bring everything into the namespace with use colored::* (see Listing 2-9).

Listing 2-9. Using the colored Crate

```
extern crate colored;
use colored::*;

//...

fn main() {
    // ...
    println!("{}", message.bright_yellow().underline()
        .on_purple());
    println!("  \\");
    println!("   \\");
    println!("    /\\_/\\");
    println!("   ( {eye} {eye} )", eye=eye.red().bold());
    println!("    =( I )=");
}
```

The colored crate defines a Colorize trait, which is implemented on a &str and String. This trait provides various chainable coloring functions:

- Coloring the text: red(), green(), blue(), etc.

- Coloring the background: on_red() (i.e., text on red background), on_green(), on_blue(), etc.

- Brighter version: bright_red(), on_bright_green(), etc.

- Styling: bold(), underline(), italic(), etc.

So Listing 2-9 will show the message in bright yellow text on a purple background, with an underline. It then makes the cat's eyes bloody red and bold. The end result is shown in Figure 2-2.

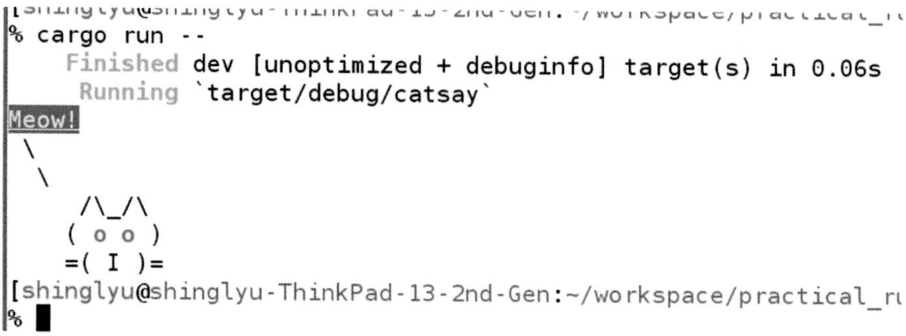

```
[shinglyu@shinglyu-ThinkPad-13-2nd-Gen:~/workspace/practical_rt
% cargo run --
    Finished dev [unoptimized + debuginfo] target(s) in 0.06s
     Running `target/debug/catsay`
Meow!
  \
   \
     /\_/\
    ( o o )
    =( I )=
[shinglyu@shinglyu-ThinkPad-13-2nd-Gen:~/workspace/practical_rt
% ▏
```

Figure 2-2. *Example output of the colored catsay*

Reading the Cat Picture from a File

Another common operation in command-line applications is reading from a file. Cowsay has a -f option that allows you to pass in a custom cow picture file. This section implements a simplified version of it to demonstrate how to read files in Rust.

First, you need to add the option for reading the file, as shown in Listing 2-10.

Listing 2-10. Adding the catfile Option

```
#[derive(StructOpt)]
struct Options {
    // ...

    #[structopt(short = "f", long = "file", parse(from_os_str))]
    /// Load the cat picture from the specified file
    catfile: Option<std::path::PathBuf>,
}
```

There are a few things to pay attention to in Listing 2-10:

- In the #[structopt(...)] annotation, the short and long version of the option (-f/--file) is named differently from the field name (catfile) in the Options struct. You can name the options and flags with user-friendly terms while keeping the variable naming consistent in the code.

- In the second part of the #[structopt(...)] annotation, you define a custom parser scheme. By default, StructOpt will use the from_str scheme, which uses the function signature fn(&str) -> T. But in this case, you are passing a string of the path name, which might be represented differently in different operating systems[5]. Therefore, you need to parse from an &OsStr instead.

---

[5]See the OsString documentation for why you need it: https://doc.rust-lang.org/std/ffi/struct.OsString.html

- The type defined for catfile is wrapped in an Option<T>. This is how you indicate that this field is optional. If the field is not provided, it will simply be an Option::None. There are other options, like Vec<T>, that represent a list of arguments, and u64 indicates that you want to count the occurrences of a parameter. For example, -v, -vv, and -vvv are commonly used to set the verbosity level.

- Inside the Option, you use a std::path::PathBuf instead of a raw string. PathBuf can help you handle paths to files more robustly because it hides many differences in how the operating systems represent paths.

Now if you run cargo run -- --help again, you'll see that a new section called OPTIONS has been added:

```
catsay 0.1.0
Shing Lyu <my@email.com>

USAGE:
    catsay [FLAGS] [OPTIONS] [message]

FLAGS:
    -d, --dead       Make the cat appears dead
    -h, --help       Prints help information
    -V, --version    Prints version information

OPTIONS:
    -f, --file <catfile> Load the cat picture from the
    specified file

ARGS:
    <message>    What does the cat say? [default: Meow!]
```

Once you have the options in place, you can use this function in the main() function to load the external file and render it (see Listing 2-11).

Listing 2-11. Reading the Catfile

```
let options = Options::from_args();

// ...

let eye = if options.dead { "x" } else { "o" };

println!("{}", message);

match &options.catfile {
    Some (path) => {
        let cat_template = std::fs::read_to_string(path)
            .expect(&format!("could not read file {:?}", path));
        let cat_picture = cat_template.replace("{eye}", eye);
        println!("{}", &cat_picture);
    },
    None => {
        // ... print the cat as before
    }
}
```

In Listing 2-11, you use a match statement to check whether the options.catfile is a Some(PathBuf) or None. If it's None, it just prints the cat as before. But if it's a Some(PathBuf), it uses std::fs::read_to_string(path) to read the file contents to a string.

An example catfile will look like Listing 2-12. To support different eyes, a placeholder {eye} is used in place of the eyes. But you can't simply use format!() to replace the eyes with o or x. This is because format!() needs to know the formatting string at compile time, but the catfile string is loaded at runtime. Therefore, you need to use the String.replace()

function to replace the eye placeholder with the actual string you are using. Alternatively, you can use libraries like strfmt[6] to have more format!-flavor code.

Listing 2-12. A Catfile

```
 \
  \                        / )
   \  (\_/)              ( (
     ) {eye} {eye}     (          ) )
   ={     Y     }=          / /
      )            '-------/ /
     (                    /
      \                   |
     ,'\             ,     ,'
     '-'\   ,    ---\    | \
        _) )         '. \ /
       (_/           ) )
                     (_/
```

Better Error Handling

Until now, you have been using unwrap() or expect() on functions that might fail, such as std::fs::read_to_string. When the return value is a Result::Err(E), unwrapping it will cause the program to crash with panic!(). This is not always desirable because you lose the ability to recover from the failure or provide a better error message so the users can figure out what happened. The human_panic crate[7] can help you produce a more human-readable panic message, but it still hard-crashes the program. A better method is to use Rust's ? operator.

---

[6]https://github.com/vitiral/strfmt
[7]https://github.com/rust-cli/human-panic

If you change std::fs::read_to_string(path).expect(...) to std::fs::read_to_string(path)? (the ? at the end is an operator, not a typo), it will be equivalent to Listing 2-13.

Listing 2-13. Pseudo-Code for an Expended Version of the ? Operator

```
// let cat_template = std::fs::read_to_string(path)?
// will be equivalent to
let cat_template = match std::fs::read_to_string(path) {
    Ok(file_content) => file_content,
    Err(e) => return e, // e: std::io::Error
};
```

The ? operator performs a match on the Result returned by read_to_string(). If the value is Ok(...), it simply unwraps the value inside it. If it's an Err(...), it early returns the Err(...). This is particularly useful when you have multiple potential points of failure in your function. Any one of them failing will cause an early return with the Err, and the function caller can then handle the error or further escalate the error to its caller.

Note   If you are familiar with the try! macro in the earlier version of Rust, you might notice that the ? operator does exactly the same thing as try!. This is because the ? operator is just syntactic sugar for try!. It was introduced in Rust 1.13.

But you might notice that the main() function returns nothing yet. By using the ? operator, the main() function might return a std::io::Error. So you have to fix the function signature to be fn main() -> Result<(), Box<dyn std::error::Error>>. You don't really care about the return value in the Ok case, so you can pass a () for it; for the Err case, you pass a weird looking Box<dyn std::error::Error>. This is a trait object, which means any type that implements the std::error::Error trait can be used here. Also don't forget to return an Ok(()) at the end of the function to satisfy the function signature (see Listing 2-14).

Listing 2-14. Changing the Function Signature to Use the ? Operator

```
fn main() -> Result<(), Box<dyn std::error::Error>> {
    // ...
    std::fs::read_to_string(path)?;
    // ...
    Ok(())
}
```

If you trigger an error now by providing a file path that doesn't exist, you'll get this not-so-user-friendly message:

```
cargo run -- -f no/such/file.txt
    Finished dev [unoptimized + debuginfo] target(s) in 0.05s
     Running 'target/debug/catsay -f no/such/file.txt'
Error: Os { code: 2, kind: NotFound, message: "No such file or
directory" }
```

If you want to provide a more user-friendly error, you can use the experimental failure crate (see Listing 2-15).

Listing 2-15. Cargo.toml for Using the failure Crate

```
[package]
// ...

[dependencies]
structopt = "0.2.15"
colored = "1.7.0"
failure = "0.1.5"
```

The failure crate provides a Context struct, which wraps the original error with a human-readable and user-facing explanation of the error, called context. This is more flexible than returning just the original Err or a String error message, because both of them are returned in a package. You can choose to look into the machine-readable error to recover or simply print the human-readable context. To use context, you can rely on the failure::ResultExt extension trait, which adds a with_context() function on result, so you can define a context message, as shown in Listing 2-16. Now the error you return actually wraps the io::Error from read_to_string() and the "could not read file filename" error message (i.e., the context).

Listing 2-16. Defining a Context on the Result Returned by read_to_string

```
// ...

use failure::ResultExt;

// ...

fn main() -> Result<(), failure::Error> {
    // ...
    std::fs::read_to_string(path)
        .with_context(|_| format!("could not read file {:?}",
            path))?
    // ...
    Ok(())
}
```

To print the context in a human-friendly way when the program exits with an error, you can use the exitfailure crate (see Listing 2-17), which is just a small wrapper for the failure::Error type (see Listing 2-18).

Listing 2-17. Cargo.toml for Using the exitfailure Crate

```
[package]
// ...

[dependencies]
structopt = "0.2.15"
colored = "1.7.0"
failure = "0.1.5"
exitfailure = "0.5.1"
```

Listing 2-18. Using exitfailure

```
// ...
use failure::ResultExt;
use exitfailure::ExitFailure;

// We return ExitFailure instead of failure:: Error
fn main() -> Result<(), ExitFailure> {
    // ...
    std::fs::read_to_string(path)
        .with_context(|_| format!(
            "could not read file {:?}",
            path
        ))?
    // ...
    Ok(())
}
```

Now the error message looks much better:

```
$ cargo run -- -f no/such/file.txt
// ... regular cargo compile output
Error: could not read file "no/such/file.txt"
Info: caused by No such file or directory (os error 2)
```

Tip   The `failure` crate and its context are much more than just printing a human-friendly error message. If you have a function call chain, you can have a nested chain of errors; each has a context that is relevant to the layer of abstraction. It also gives ergonomic ways to manipulate the chain of errors and backtraces. It also allows easier downcasting from a generic `Error` to a specific `Fail` type, compared to the built-in `std::error::Error`. It's worth considering using `failure` if your command-line program grows more and more complex.

Piping to Other Commands

Piping is one of the most powerful features of UNIX-like operating systems, in which the output of one command can be sent directly to another command as input. This allows command-line programs to be designed in a modular way and work together easily. To make the `catsay` tool pipe-friendly, you need to take care of the input and output formats.

Piping to STDOUT Without Color

You already learned how to print separately to STDOUT and STDERR. Normally, you pipe the STDOUT to another program as input. But you also added colors to the output. The way coloring works is that you add ANSI color escape codes to the output, and the terminal will interpret that color code and apply the color to the text. You can see the raw color codes by piping the output to a file with `cargo run > output.txt`. The contents of the `output.txt` file will look like Listing 2-19.

Listing 2-19. Raw Color Escaped Code

```
^[[4;45;93mMeow!^[[0m
\
 \
     /\_/\
    ( ^[[1;31mo^[[0m ^[[1;31mo^[[0m )
    =( I )=
```

Although many tools can handle these codes properly, some might still fail to recognize these color codes and treat them as raw characters. To avoid this kind of situation, you can set the NO_COLOR environment variable to 1 to turn off the coloring. This NO_COLOR environment variable is an informal standard[8] that toggles coloring on and off. The colored crate and many other command-line tools or libraries have already implemented this standard.

If you run NO_COLOR=1 cargo run, you'll see there is no color anymore. If you pipe the output to a file, you'll also notice that the color code is no longer present. This should come in handy if you want to pipe colored output to other command-line programs.

---

[8]https://no-color.org/

Accepting STDIN

Taking input from STDIN is another way to interact with other programs. You can make catsay take a string from STDIN as the message argument. You create a switch called --stdin that enables this behavior:

```
cat "Hello world" | catsay --stdin
```

You can then add one flag called --stdin to the struct:

```
#[derive(StructOpt)]
struct Options {
    // ...
    #[structopt(short = "i", long = "stdin")]
    /// Read the message from STDIN instead of the argument
    stdin: bool,
}
```

Then in the main() function, whenever you see that the options.stdin is true, you need to read the message from STDIN. Otherwise, you'll keep the old behavior and read from the options.message argument. The code is illustrated in Listing 2-20. Notice that use std::io and std::io::Read are used on [2] to read the STDIN into a string. The read_to_string() function does not return a string. Instead, it fills the &mut String argument passed to it. Because it has to be mutable, you have to add a mut on [1].

Listing 2-20. Reading from STDIN

```
// ...
use std::io::{self, Read};

fn main() -> Result<(), ExitFailure> {
    let options = Options::from_args();
    let mut message = String::new(); // [1]
```

```
if options.stdin {
    io::stdin().read_to_string(&mut message)?; // [2]
} else {
    message = options.message;
};

// print the message and cat picture...
}
```

This allows you to read the message from the standard input. Being able to interact with other programs through piping will make your program much more flexible and expandable.

Integration Testing

Automated testing is a vital tool for improving code quality. This chapter has touched on quite a few ways to implement features in your program, but it hasn't yet mentioned how to test these features. You have been writing everything in the main() function in the main.rs file. But that's not very testable.

To unit test the business logic, it's better to split the functionality into a separate crate and let the main.rs file import and use that crate. Then you can unit test the other crate, which contains the business logic. These kinds of unit tests are relatively easy to write; you can follow the official Rust documentation or any introductory Rust book/course to learn how to unit test your code. This section focuses on how to write an integration test that is specific to command-line programs.

Testing a command-line program usually involves running the command and then verifying its return code and STDOUT/STDERR output. This can be easily done by writing a shell script. But writing a shell script means that you have to implement your own assertion and test the result aggregation and reporting, which Rust already supports in its unit testing framework. So you are going to use the std::process::Command and assert_cmd[9] crate to test the program in Rust.

First, create a folder called tests in the project's root directory and then create a file named integration_test.rs, as shown in Listing 2-21. You also need to add the assert_cmd crate to Cargo.toml (see Listing 2-22).

Listing 2-21. A Basic Smoke Test

```rust
use std::process::Command;   // Run programs
use assert_cmd::prelude::*; // Add methods on commands

#[test]
fn run_with_defaults()
    -> Result<(), Box<dyn std::error::Error>> {
    Command::cargo_bin("catsay")
        .expect("binary exists")
        .assert()
        .success();

    Ok(())
}
```

Listing 2-22. Cargo.toml for Using assert_cmd

```toml
[package]
// ...

[dependencies]
// ...
predicates = "1.0.0"
```

---

[9]https://crates.io/crates/assert_cmd

This example uses two crates, the `std::process::Command` and `assert_cmd::prelude::*`. The `std::process::Command` crate gives you a `Command` struct that can help you run a program in a newly spawned process. The `assert_cmd::prelude::*` module imports a few useful traits that extend `Command` to be more suitable for integration testing, like `cargo_bin()`, `assert()` and `success()`.

In the main test function `run_with_defaults()`, you first initialize the command using `Command::cargo_bin`, which takes a Cargo-built binary name (in this case, it's `catsay`). You then use `expect()` to handle cases such as when the binary doesn't exist, which will return an `Err(CargoError)`. Then you call `assert()` on the command, which produces an `Assert` struct, on which you can run various assertions of the status and output of the executed command. You only run a very basic assertion `success()`, which checks if the command succeeded or not.

You can run this test with `cargo test`, and you should get output like Listing 2-23.

Listing 2-23. Example Output of a Cargo Test Run

```
$ cargo test
zsh: correct 'test' to 'tests' [nyae]? n
   Compiling catsay v0.1.0
    Finished dev [unoptimized + debuginfo] target(s) in 1.04s
      Running   target/debug/deps/catsay-bf24a9cbada6cbf2

running 0 tests

test result: ok. 0 passed; 0 failed; 0 ignored; 0 measured; 0
filtered out

      Running   target/debug/deps/integration_test-
      cce770f212f0b7be
```

```
running  1  test
test run_with_defaults ... ok
```

```
test result: ok. 1 passed; 0 failed; 0 ignored; 0 measured;
0 filtered out
```

The test you just wrote was not very exciting, nor did it test much more than making sure the code runs. The next step you can take is to check the STDOUT and see if it contains the expected output. When you call the catsay program without an argument, it prints out a cat saying "Meow!", so you can verify if there is the string "Meow!" in the standard output. To do this, you use the stdout() function from assert_cmd, and to check for the string, you use the predicates module (see Listing 2-24) to build a predicate that checks for the string, as shown in Listing 2-25.

Listing 2-24. Cargo.toml for Using Predicates

```
[package]
// ...

[dependencies]
// ...
assert_cmd  =  "0.11.1"
predicates  =  "1.0.0"
```

Listing 2-25. Check that the STDOUT Contains a Certain String

```
// ...
use predicates::prelude::*; // Used for writing assertions

#[test]
fn run_with_defaults()
    -> Result<(), Box<dyn std::error::Error>> {
    Command::cargo_bin("catsay")
        .expect("binary exists")
```

```
        .assert()
        .success()
        .stdout(predicate::str::contains("Meow!"));
    Ok(())
}
```

You can test not only positive cases but also test negative cases and error handling. For example, Listing 2-26 checks whether the program will handle an invalid -f argument correctly.

Listing 2-26. Check that a Bad Argument Triggers a Failure

```
#[test]
fn fail_on_non_existing_file()
    -> Result<(), Box<std::error::Error>> {
    Command::cargo_bin("catsay")
        .expect("binary exists")
        .args(&["-f", "no/such/file.txt"])
        .assert()
        .failure();
    Ok(())
}
```

You pass an invalid file no/such/file.txt to the -f argument using the .args() function. This is equivalent to calling catsay -f no/such/file.txt. You expect that the program will exit with an error because it fails to read the file. Therefore, you call .assert().failure() to check if it actually fails.

Publishing and Distributing the Program

So once you are happy with your program, you'll want to package it so anyone can easily install it and use it as a command in their shell. There are several ways you can do this; each method has some tradeoffs between the effort on the user's side (easy to install) and the effort on the author's side (easy to build and package).

Install from Source

If you run `cargo install --path ./` in the project folder, you can see Cargo compiling the code in release mode, then "install" it into the `/.cargo/bin` folder. You can then append this path to the PATH environment variable, and the `catsay` command should be available in the shell.

Tip   The location where Cargo installs your program can be overridden by setting the CARGO_HOME environment variable. By default, it's set to $HOME/`.cargo`.

You can publish the code to any public code hosting service, like GitHub or Bitbucket. You can even publish a tarball and then ask your users to download the source code and run `cargo install --path ./`. But there are several drawbacks to this method:

- It's hard for the users to find your program.

- It requires knowledge on how to download the source code and compile it.

- The user needs the full Rust toolchain and a powerful computer to compile the source code.

Publish to crates.io

Nowadays, most Rust programmers search packages on `crates.io`. So to make your program easier to find, you can publish it to `crates.io`. It's very easy to publish a program on `crates.io`, and users can easily run `cargo install <crate name>` to download and install it.

To be able to publish on `crates.io`, you need to have an account and get an access token. Here are the steps to acquire one:

1. Go to `https://crates.io`.

2. Click Log in with GitHub. (You need a GitHub account.)

3. Once you're logged in, click on your username and select Account Settings.

4. Under the API Access section, you can generate a token. Copy that token and keep it handy.

Once you have the token, you can run `cargo login <token>` (replace `<token>` with the token you just created.) to allow Cargo to access `crates.io` on your behalf. Then you can run `cargo package`, which will package your program into a format that `crates.io` accepts. You can check the `target/package` folder to see what was generated. Once the package is ready, simply run `cargo publish` to publish it to `crates.io`.

Keep in mind that once the code is uploaded to `crates.io`, it stays there forever and can't be removed or overwritten. To update the code, you need to increase the version number in `Cargo.toml` and publish a new version. If you accidentally publish a broken version, you can use the `cargo yank` command to "yank" it. That means no new dependencies can be created against that version, but existing ones will still work. And even though the version is yanked, the code still stays public. So never publish any secret (e.g., password, access token, or personal information) in your `crates.io` package.

Although publishing to `crates.io` solves the discoverability issue and takes away the burden on the users to manually download your code, the code is still compiled from scratch every time a user installs it. So the user still needs to have the full Rust toolchain installed on their machine. To make it even easier for the users, you can precompile the project into binaries and release them directly.

Building Binaries for Distribution

Rust compiles to native code and, by default, links statically, so it doesn't require a heavy runtime like a Java Virtual Machine or a Python interpreter. If you run `cargo build --release`, Cargo will compile your program in release mode, which means a higher level of optimization and less verbose logging than the default debug mode. You'll find the built binary in `target/release/catsay`. This binary can then be sent to users using the same platform as you, and they can execute it directly without installing anything.

Notice that I said "using the same platform". This is because the binary might not run on another CPU architecture and operating system combination. In theory, you can do a cross-compilation to compile your binary for a different target platform. For example, if you are running a Linux machine with x86_64 CPU, you can compile it for an iPhone running on an ARM processor. This usually requires you to install cross-compilers and linkers, which might be tedious to set up on your own machine. But thankfully, the `cross`[10] project solves this problem by wrapping all the cross-compilation environments into Docker images. This spins up a lightweight virtual machine in Docker, with all the cross-compilation toolchain and libraries configured to cross-compile the most portable binaries.

However, `cross` only works on x86_64 Linux machines. If you don't want to set up a Linux machine with Docker just for the compilation, you can easily offload that task to a hosted continuous integration (CI) service.

---

[10]`https://github.com/rust-embedded/cross`

Nowadays, you can easily get free access to CI services like Travis CI and AppVeyor (for Windows) and connect them with GitHub. The trust[11] project provides templates to set up Travis CI and AppVeyor CI pipelines to build your binaries. For Linux builds, it actually uses cross underneath. For Windows builds, it relies on the Windows-based AppVeyor CI.

Once the binaries are built, you can put the binaries online for users to download. But usually, different platforms have their specific package formats, which come with package repositories and package managers. Users can effortlessly search, download, install, and update binaries using them. For example, MacOS has Homebrew Formulae, Debian has Deb, and Red Hat Linux has RPM. It's a good idea to submit your program to each package repository for discoverability and easier updates. But different platforms have different ways of packaging and submission, so they are not covered in this book. You can find tools on crates.io to help you pack for a specific format—for example, cargo-deb and cargo-rpm.

Conclusion

This chapter talked about how to build a command-line program in Rust. It started with how to create a binary project and read simple command-line arguments. Then you saw how to improve the command-line parser and started to parse more complex arguments with StructOpt. You looked at how to add positional arguments, binary flags, and options; and how to add description and default values to them. You also learned how to build common command-line features like coloring, reading from a file, and accepting standard input and output to standard output and standard error. Then you saw how to run integration tests on a command-line program. Finally, you learned about various ways to publish and distribute your program.

---

[11]https://github.com/japaric/trust

CHAPTER 3

Creating Graphical User Interfaces (GUIs)

Command-line tools are handy when you need small tools that don't require visual interaction or batch processing. But a command-line program's user interface is usually limited to text input/output and files. This is sometimes not sufficient when 2D (or even 3D) visual interaction is required. So this chapter breaks out of the constraint of the command-line interface and talks about graphical user interfaces (GUIs).

The end goal of this chapter is to show you how to build cross-platform desktop applications. Although there are frameworks like Electron[1], which allows you to build a desktop app in HTML, CSS, and JavaScript, they actually wrap a browser engine inside. Therefore the developer experience will be closer to building a website or web app, not like coding a native desktop application. You'll use a framework that showcases the experience of building a native application in Rust.

As a bridge between command-line programs and actual GUI apps, I'll introduce the text-based user interface (TUI). A TUI looks like a GUI, but it's drawn with text characters. Thus it can be created in a terminal environment. But because it's drawn with text characters, the resolution is very low, and the screen real estate is very limited. Nevertheless, TUI is a good way to understand the high-level concept of event-driven

---

[1]https://electronjs.org/

© Shing Lyu 2020
S. Lyu, *Practical Rust Projects*, https://doi.org/10.1007/978-1-4842-5599-5_3

architecture that is common in GUI programs. Once you acquire the knowledge of how a TUI program is structured, you'll apply that knowledge to implement a full-fledged GUI program.

What Are You Building?

To avoid distractions from complex business logic, you'll be building a simplified version of the catsay program in TUI and GUI. For TUI, you'll build:

- An interactive form to receive the message. (see Figure 3-1)

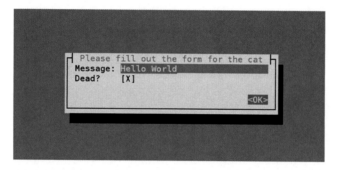

Figure 3-1. *The input form of the TUI program*

- An optional checkbox for the --dead option.

- Once the user clicks OK, a dialog box will pop up and show a cat saying the message (see Figure 3-2).

You'll then move on to building a GUI that has the same input as the TUI program. But this time, instead of the ASCII art cat, you'll show a picture of a real cat (see Figure 3-3).

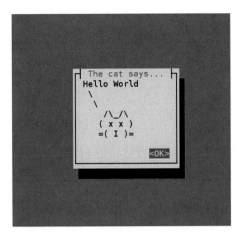

Figure 3-2. *An example of the TUI program*

Figure 3-3. *An example of the GUI program*

You'll be building the GUI using gtk-rs, which is a Rust binding for the GTK+ 3 library and its underlying libraries. You'll first build the GUI in pure Rust code, and then you'll see how to use Glade, a user interface

45

design tool that can help you design the layout in a more intuitive and easy-to-manage way. There are many other GUI libraries and frameworks out there; I discuss why I chose gtk-rs in the section titled "Other Alternatives".

Building a Text-Based User Interface

You built a command-line tool in Chapter 2 and you used println!() for most of the output. The problem with it is that you can only output one line at a time. Although you can create some kind of ASCII art image by carefully aligning the lines you print, it won't really scale if you want to draw windows, dialog boxes, and buttons, not to mention handle keyboard input and mouse clicks. Thankfully, some libraries can help you build UI components easily. They are known as "text-based user interface" libraries. One example is the ncurses library for UNIX-like systems. Ncurses stands for "new curses" because it was the "new" (in the 1990s) version of the old curses library in System V Release 4.0 (SVr4). You'll be using the Cursive crate, which uses ncurses by default. I'll discuss other alternatives at the end of the chapter, but I chose Cursive because it hides many low-level details, so it's very easy to work with.

You'll be using the default ncurses backend for simplicity, but if you need cross-system support for Windows and/or MacOS, you can choose other backends like pancurses or crossterm. To use ncurses, you need to install it on your system. For Ubuntu, simply run the following in the shell:

```
sudo apt-get install libncursesw5-dev
```

Then you can create a new project with cargo new and add the Cursive crate to Cargo.toml:

```
[dependencies]
cursive = "0.11.2"
```

In the src/main.rs file, you can write the minimal code shown in Listing 3-1.

Listing 3-1. Basic Skeleton Code for Cursive TUI

```
extern crate cursive;

use cursive::Cursive;

fn main() {
    let mut siv = Cursive::default();

    siv.run(); // starting the event loop
}
```

This will create a Cursive root object with Cursive::default() and start the event loop with siv.run(). The event loop is a fundamental concept in building user interfaces. For a command-line program, interactions are usually limited to one input and one output. If you need to take user input, you have to pause the execution of the program and wait for the user input to finish. No other operations or output can be processed at that time.

But a GUI might be expecting multiple inputs, for example, keypresses or mouse clicks on any of the many buttons on a program's user interface. Since you can't predict which input will be triggered first, the program (conceptually) runs in an infinite loop that handles whatever next input is triggered. If you have registered some event handler, the event loop will invoke the handler when the event happens. For example, if you have an OK button in a dialog box, clicking it will trigger a button click event, which might be handled by a handler that closes this dialog box.

Showing a Dialog Box

If you now run `cargo run`, you can see a blue screen (see Figure 3-4). But that's not very exciting. To display the cat ASCII art on the screen you just created, you need to add the code in Listing 3-2 to `main.rs`.

Figure 3-4. *An empty cursive screen*

Listing 3-2. Showing a TextView

```
extern crate cursive;

use cursive::Cursive;
use cursive::views::TextView; // Import the TextView

fn main() {
    let mut siv = Cursive::default();
    let cat_text = "Meow!
```

```
    \\
     \\
       /\\_/\\
      ( o o )
      =( I )=";

      // Declaring the app layout
      siv.add_layer(TextView::new(cat_text));

      siv.run();
}
```

Notice that before the event loop starts, you set up the content of the app with the following:

```
siv.add_layer(TextView::new(cat_text));
```

The TextView holds the cat ASCII art. Views are the main building blocks of a Cursive TUI program. There are many pre-built views in the cursive::views module; for example, buttons, checkboxes, dialogs, progress bars, etc. You can also implement custom views by implementing the View trait. The TextView is used to hold fixed text, which you passed in as a constructor parameter. But the newly created TextView is not visible yet because it is not part of the main program. You can add it as a layer to the main Cursive program you just created by using siv.add_layer(). Cursive uses layers to create a stacked view of the components (i.e., Views). Layers are stacked together so that the top-most one will be active and can receive input. They are also rendered with a shadow, so they look like 3D layers stacked together. You can see how that looks like in Figure 3-5.

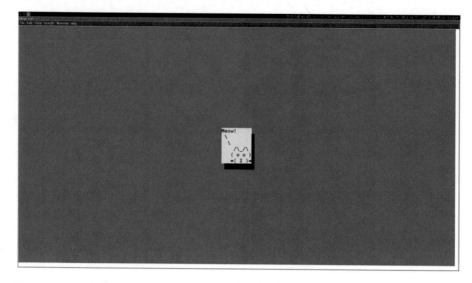

Figure 3-5. *A TextView showing the cat*

Handling Simple Keyboard Inputs

Up until now, this TUI program produces output but can't handle any input. To close the program, you have to press Ctrl+C to send an interrupt signal to force-terminate it. You can try to make the program respond to the ESC keypress and close the program gracefully by calling `Cursive.quit()`. Modify the code to resemble Listing 3-3.

Listing 3-3. Listen for an ESC Key to Close the Program

```
// ...
use cursive::event::Key;

fn main() {
    let mut siv = Cursive::default();
    let cat_text = // ...
```

```
siv.add_layer(TextView::new(cat_text));

// Listen to Key::Esc and quit
siv.add_global_callback(Key::Esc, |s| s.quit());

siv.run();
}
```

In the code, you set up a global callback with `siv.add_global_callback()`. This function takes two arguments: an event and a callback function (cb). Whenever an event occurs, the callback function (closure) will be executed. You assign `cursive::event::Key::Esc` as the event, which is triggered when the ESC key is pressed. In the callback argument, you pass a closure `|s| s.quit()`. The s is a mutable reference to the `Cursive` struct itself, so `s.quit()` will gracefully quit the program.

The closure you created does not get executed right away, nor does the `siv.add_global_callback()` function block the execution until a key is pressed. The line simply registers the callback and continues the execution of the program. When the next line, `siv.run()`, is executed, the event loop starts and waits for keypresses and mouse clicks. By using a non-blocking event-based system, the user interface becomes more responsive to user input, and you are not limited to one kind of interaction at a time. You can set up multiple event handlers so they can handle different kinds of events regardless of the order. You'll see more event handlers in the coming sections.

Adding a Dialog

The user interface you just created still feels a little rough around the edges. To give the program a more sophisticated look and feel, you can wrap the `TextView` with a `Dialog` (see Listing 3-4).

Listing 3-4. Displaying a Dialog

```
extern crate cursive;

use cursive::views::{Dialog, TextView};
use cursive::Cursive;

fn main() {
    let mut siv = Cursive::default();
    let cat_text = // ...

    siv.add_layer(
        Dialog::around(TextView::new(cat_text))
            .button("OK", |s| s.quit())
    );

    siv.run();
}
```

You use `Dialog::around()` to wrap the `TextView`. This will wrap the `TextView` inside the `Dialog`. You can also add a button to the dialog with a label (`"OK"`) and a callback (`|s| s.quit()`). This callback will be triggered when the button is clicked. One nice feature about `Cursive` is that it supports keyboard and mouse interactions out-of-box, so you can close the program by either pressing the Enter (Return) key or double-clicking the OK button with the mouse (see Figure 3-6).

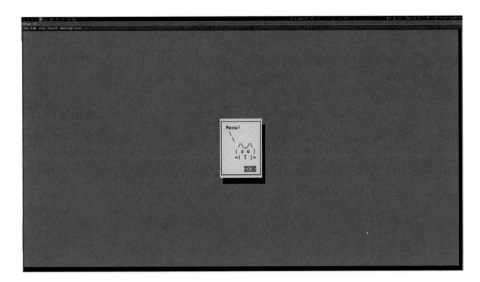

Figure 3-6. *Displaying a dialog with an OK button*

Multi-Step Dialogs

You are not limited to one static layer at a time. You can actually build a multi-step flow. In the first step, the user is prompted to fill in a form and press OK, at which point you hide the form and display the cat pictures using the information provided in the form. You can implement this, as shown in Listing 3-5.

Listing 3-5. Multi-Step Form

```
extern crate cursive;

use cursive::traits::Identifiable; // for .with_id()
                                   // and .call_on_id()
use cursive::views::{Checkbox, Dialog, EditView, ListView,
    TextView};
use cursive::Cursive;
```

```
// wrap all form fields value in one struct so we can pass
// around easily
struct CatsayOptions<'a> {
    message: &'a str,
    dead: bool,
}

fn input_step(siv: &mut Cursive) {
    siv.add_layer(
        Dialog::new()
            .title("Please fill out the form for the cat")
            // setting the title
            .content(
                ListView::new()
                    .child(
                        "Message:",
                        EditView::new().with_id("message")
                    )
                    .child(
                        "Dead?",
                        Checkbox::new().with_id("dead")
                    ),
            )
            .button("OK", |s| {
                let message = s
                    .call_on_id(
                        "message",
                        |t: &mut EditView| t.get_content()
                    ).unwrap();
                let is_dead = s
                    .call_on_id(
                        "dead",
```

```rust
                    |t: &mut Checkbox| t.is_checked()
                ).unwrap();
            let options = CatsayOptions {
                message: &message,
                dead: is_dead,
            };
            result_step(s, &options) // [2]
        }),
    );
}

fn result_step(siv: &mut Cursive, options: &CatsayOptions) {
    let eye = if options.dead { "x" } else { "o" };

    let cat_text = format!(

        "{msg}
  \\
   \\
    /\\_/\\
   ( {eye} {eye} )
   =( I )=",
        msg = options.message,
        eye = eye
    );

    siv.pop_layer(); // [3]
    siv.add_layer(   // [4]
        Dialog::around(TextView::new(cat_text))
            .title("The cat says...")
            .button("OK", |s| s.quit()),
    );
}
```

55

```
fn main() {
    let mut siv = Cursive::default();

    input_step(&mut siv); // [1]

    siv.run();
}
```

This example is slightly more complex, so I'll break it down a little bit. First, let's walk through the high-level flow. In the main() function, instead of directly setting up the layout with add_layer(), you move all the layout code into the input_step(&mut siv) function ([1]). Inside input_step, you set up a form, which I'll discuss in detail later. Notice that it has a button called OK. In the callback function of the button, you call result_step(s, &options)([2]), which handles the next step. In result_step(), you first hide the form by calling siv.pop_layer() ([3]). This "pops" the existing layer (i.e., the form layer) from the layers stack, and then you add your layer that displays the cat in a TextView ([4]). So the flow is as follows:

- main(): Create the Cursive object and call input_step().

- input_step(): Set up the form layout and callbacks.

- result_step(): When OK is clicked, hide the form and show the cat dialog.

Reading User Input

Now you understand how the program goes from one layer to another, but how does the user's input (the message and the "Dead?" flag) get carried from the form to the cat picture dialog? If you take a closer look at the input_step() in Listing 3-5, you can see that the step consists of two parts. First, you set up the input fields:

```
siv.add_layer(
    Dialog::new()
        .title("Please fill out the form for the cat")
        // setting the title
        .content(
            ListView::new()
                .child(
                    "Message:",
                    EditView::new().with_id("message")
                )
                .child(
                    "Dead?",
                    Checkbox::new().with_id("dead")
                ),
        )
    )
```

As before, you create a layer and add a Dialog element to it. You set the content of the Dialog using .content() . Inside the Dialog, you create two input elements, an EditView and a Checkbox. In order to place them properly, you wrap them in a ListView, which is a layout container that will display its children in a scrollable list. Notice that you call .with_id() on the EditView and Checkbox. This gives each of them a unique ID, which you can use to identify and retrieve them later.

Then you add a button to the Dialog like so:

```
Dialog::new()
    .title(...)
    .content(...)
    .button("OK", |s| {
        let message = s
            .call_on_id(
                "message",
                |t: &mut EditView| t.get_content()
```

```
            ).unwrap();
        let is_dead = s
            .call_on_id(
                "dead",
                |t: &mut Checkbox| t.is_checked()
            ).unwrap();
        let options = CatsayOptions {
            message: &message,
            dead: is_dead,
        };
        result_step(s, &options)
    }),
```

In this button's callback, you read the message and the status of the
"Dead?" flag, collect them into a CatsayOptions struct, then pass the
CatsayOptions struct to the result_step() to display the final output.
This is when the IDs come in handy. The first argument ("message") of the
s.call_on_id() call is the ID you just set. call_on_id() will try to find
the element and pass its mutable reference into the callback closure (the
second argument). Inside the closure you use t.get_content() (where
t is &mut EditView) to get the text inside the EditView. You might fail to
find any element with the given ID, so call_on_id() returns an Option
wrapping the return value of the closure. That's why you have to unwrap
it to get the actual string. You did something similar for the Checkbox.
By calling is_checked() on Checkbox it will return a Boolean indicating
whether the checkbox is checked or not.

Then you simply wrap the two values into a CatsayOptions struct,
so you can pass it to the result_step(). Inside the result_step() (see
Listing 3-5), you display the cat ASCII art in a Dialog using the options
from the previous step.

There are many more callbacks and UI patterns you can use. But TUI is relatively limited due to its low resolution. There is very limited space on the screen if you have to render each pixel as a character. Also, it's not very aesthetically pleasing for modern users, and is sometimes even a little bit intimidating. However, TUI is still very useful if you want to build some small tools that require simple interactions. Also, it might be useful on remote servers where users need to SSH in remotely. Due to these limitations, I am going to conclude this journey in TUI and move on to GUI, the graphical user interface.

Moving to Graphical User Interfaces (GUIs)

In the next half of this chapter, you'll be building a GUI version of the TUI program you just built. This time you'll be able to actually render a cat photo! For this purpose, you are going to use the gtk-rs crate, which is a Rust binding for the GTK library. GTK, originally known as GTK+ and GIMP Toolkit, is a free and open-source widget toolkit for building GUIs. It is written in C and supports multiple platforms like Linux, Microsoft Windows, and MacOS. It provides many UI widgets out-of-the-box so you can easily assemble a GUI program. Many popular programs like the GNOME desktop environment use it.

There are many other GUI toolkits for Rust, but I chose gtk-rs for its popularity and maturity. It's one of the most downloaded GUI crates on crates.io, and it is one of the most mature libraries in the domain because of the maturity of GTK itself. It can potentially support cross-platform development (by installing GTK libraries for the target platform). An additional benefit of using gtk-rs is the great documentation and community support from the original GTK library. Because it's a binding around the C-based GTK library, whenever the Rust documentation is not clear, you can always check the C documentation and many discussions online. I discuss the other alternatives in the section titled "Other Alternatives".

Creating a Window

First, try to create a window with GTK. gtk-rs relies on the system GTK library. To install it on Ubuntu[2], simply run

```
sudo apt-get install libgtk-3-dev
```

Then, create a new project with cargo new and add the following dependency to Cargo.toml:

```
[dependencies]
gio = "0.6.0" # the underlying GLib bindings

[dependencies.gtk]
version = "0.6.0"  # the gtk crate version
features = ["v3_22"]  # system gtk version
```

This is slightly more complex than the Cargo dependencies you've seen. Because gtk-rs relies on the system gtk library, it uses the Cargo "feature" to control which version of the system gtk library it is targeting. So version = "0.6.0" is specifying the version of the gtk-rs crate itself, while v3_18 is the version of the system gtk library you are using. In case you don't know which version of the system gtk library you've installed, you can run dpkg -l libgtk-3-0 to find out.

You now have done the groundwork and are ready to code. Create a src/main.rs file and copy Listing 3-6 into it.

Listing 3-6. Opening a GTK Window

```
extern crate gio;
extern crate gtk;
```

---

[2]You can find installation instructions for other platforms at https://gtk-rs.org/docs-src/requirements.html.

```rust
use gio::prelude::*;
use gtk::prelude::*;
use gtk::{Application, ApplicationWindow};
use std::env;

fn main() {
    let app = Application::new(
        "com.shinglyu.catsay-gui",
        gio::ApplicationFlags::empty ()
    ).expect("Failed to initialize GTK.");

    app.connect_startup(|app| {
        let window = ApplicationWindow::new(app);
        window.set_title("Catsay");
        window.set_default_size(350, 70);

        window.connect_delete_event(|win, _| {
            win.destroy();
            Inhibit(false) // Don't prevent the default
            behavior (i.e. close)
        });

        window.show_all();
    });

    app.connect_activate(|_| {});
    app.run(&env::args().collect::<Vec<_>>());
}
```

You might notice that the code has a very similar structure to the TUI program. First, you create a GTK application using Application::new. You have to set an application ID in the first argument. GTK uses a "reverse DNS" style for ID. So let's say the application will have a public website at https://catsay-gui.shinglyu.com. In that case, you should use com.shinglyu.catsay-gui for the ID. When the application starts, the startup event is triggered. You should set up the application inside the startup event handler. In this case, you create an ApplicationWindow and set its title and size. You also register an event handler for the delete event, in which you destroy the window (win.destroy()). This will be triggered when you try to close the window. Finally, you run window.show_all() so the window does not remain hidden when the application starts.

After startup, the application will receive an activate event. This is usually when you show a default new window. For example, a word processor might open a new empty document. But since this application does not require such a step, you simply pass an empty closure that does nothing. Finally, you run app.run() to start the event loop. You also pass all the command-line arguments env::args() to the application in case you need them later in the application.

Note   Notice that a weird-looking Inhibit(false) is returned in the delete event handler. Sometimes you don't want the default event handler to work. For example, when the user tries to close the window, you want to ask for a confirmation before it closes. You have to stop the event from propagating to the default event handler because it will close the window right away. If you return Inhibit(true), GTK will stop propagating the event to the default handler. But in this example, you do want the window to be closed, so you simply return Inhibit(false).

Now if you run cargo run, the empty window shown in Figure 3-7 will appear.

Figure 3-7. *An empty GTK window*

Displaying an Image

Now add a few lines to show a cat image in the window by adding the code in Listing 3-7 to main().

Listing 3-7. Showing Text and a Cat Picture

```
use gtk::{Application, ApplicationWindow, Box, Image, Label,
    Orientation};
// ...

fn main() {
    // ...

    app.connect_startup(|app| {
        let window = ApplicationWindow::new(app);

        // ... set up window title, size and delete_event

        let layout_box = Box::new(Orientation::Vertical, 0);
        // [1]

        let label = Label::new("Meow!\n     \\\n     \\");

        layout_box.add(&label);

        let cat_image = Image::new_from_file(
            "./images/cat.png"
        ); // [2]
        layout_box.add(&cat_image);

        window.add(&layout_box); // [3]

        window.show_all();
    });

    // ...
}
```

You are trying to display text (Label) and an image (Image). But to properly display the two together, you wrap them in a GtkBox. A GtkBox is a container that can display widgets in a single row or column. In [1], you create a box with Orientation::Vertical, which will display the widgets from top to down in a vertical column. The second parameter, 0, is the spacing between each widget, which is set to none.

Then you create the text in a Label, which is similar to TextView in the TUI example. You also create an Image using Image::new_from_file("./ images/cat.png"). This creates a GTK image widget that shows a PNG file. Then you'll create a folder in the same project called images and put the cat.png image in there. These two elements are not showing yet, and you have to add them to the container with layout_box.add(&label) and layout_box.add(&cat_image), then add the layout box to the window (window.add(&layout box)). The result will look like Figure 3-8.

Figure 3-8. *Displaying the text and text image in GTK*

Tip   This example defined the layout of the widgets in the Rust code. But sometimes, when the widgets are positioned incorrectly, it's pretty hard to figure out why they went astray just by reading the code. The good news is that GTK provides a visual debugger so you can see the widget tree and have the widgets highlighted in the application window. Simply run your GTK application with the environment variable GTK_DEBUG set to `interactive`. For example, `GTK_ DEBUG=interactive cargo run`. You'll see the program starts along with the debugger window (see Figure 3-9). In the Objects tab in the debugger, you can see the hierarchy of the widgets. If you click on one of the widgets, that widget will flash in the main application window to show its position and size. In Figure 3-10 you select the `GtkLabel` widget, and you can see it is being highlighted. This can help you debug and tweak the layout of the widgets much easier.

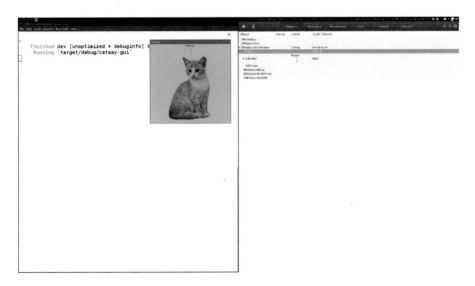

Figure 3-9. *GTK debugger that highlights the GtkBox*

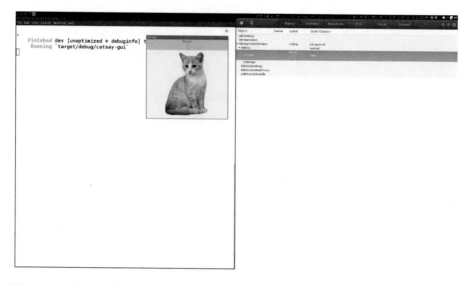

Figure 3-10. *GTK debugger that highlights the GtkLabel*

Using Glade to Design the UI

Listing 3-7 built the UI procedurally. That means you have to create widgets, put them in containers, put containers into bigger containers, then attach them to the window, and finally display them, all using Rust code. When the program grows larger and larger, this way of working is very error-prone and hard to visualize. An alternative way is to define the UI layout declaratively. Instead, build the UI like so:

- Create a GtkBox

- Create a GtkLabel

- Put the GtkLabel in the GtkBox

- Create a GtkImage

- Put the GtkImage in the GtkBox

- Put the GtkBox in the window

You can declare that you want a layout that follows this structure:

- `window`
  - `GtkBox`
    - `GtkLabel`
    - `GtkImage`

GTK provides a way to make the declaration by using XML (eXtensible Markup Language) markup. The XML file contains the static declaration of the layout of the widgets and can be loaded using the `GTKBuilder` object. The UI can be built in runtime. If you write your example application in the previous section in the XML format, it will look like Listing 3-8. You can clearly see a hierarchy of a `GtkBox` containing a `GtkLabel` and a `GtkImage`.

Listing 3-8. An Example of Glade XML

```
<?xml version="1.0" encoding="UTF-8"?>
<interface>
  <requires lib="gtk+" version="3.12"/>
  <object class="GtkApplicationWindow" id="applicationwindow1">
    <child>
      <object class="GtkBox" id="box1">
        <property name="orientation">vertical</property>
        <child>
          <object class="GtkLabel" id="label1">
            <property name="label" translatable="yes">Meow!
            </property>
          </object>
        </child>
        <child>
          <object class="GtkImage" id="image1">
            <property name="pixbuf">./images/cat.png</property>
          </object>
```

```
        </child>
      </object>
    </child>
  </object>
</interface>
```

But writing this XML by hand is very tedious. You can use Glade (see Figure 3-11), the UI design tool that comes with GTK, to generate the XML. You can install Glade with the command: sudo apt-get install glade. In Glade, you can drag and drop widgets in a WYSIWYG (What-You-See-Is-What-You-Get) editor. You can also tweak the parameters of individual widgets and get instant feedback. With Glade (and the XML layout definition), you can separate the concern of the visual presentation from the action and behavior. You can keep most of the visual design and layout in the XML and leave only event handlers logic in the Rust code.

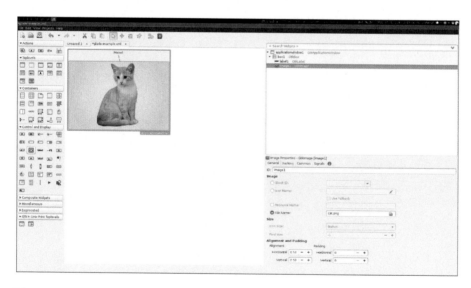

Figure 3-11. *Glade UI design tool*

You learn how to build a simple form with Glade as the foundation to demonstrate input events and handlers in the following sections. You can drag and drop a form that looks like Figure 3-12; its widgets are organized as shown in Figure 3-13. Then, click the File menu and choose Save As to save this to an XML file called layout.glade (shown in Listing 3-9).

Figure 3-12.   *Building the form with Glade*

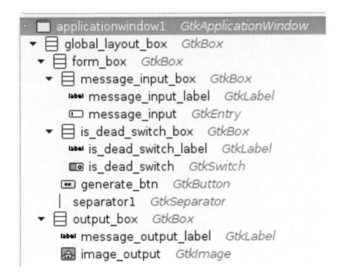

Figure 3-13.   *Widget hierarchy of the form*

Listing 3-9. Glade Layout XML

```xml
<?xml version="1.0" encoding="UTF-8"?>
<!-- Generated with glade 3.18.3 -->
<interface>
  <requires lib="gtk+" version="3.12"/>
  <object class="GtkApplicationWindow" id="applicationwindow1">
    <property name="can_focus">False</property>
    <property name="title" translatable="yes">Catsay</property>
    <child>
      <object class="GtkBox" id="global_layout_box">
        <property name="visible">True</property>
        <property name="can_focus">False</property>
        <property name="orientation">vertical</property>
        <child>
          <object class="GtkBox" id="form_box">
            <property name="visible">True</property>
            <property name="can_focus">False</property>
            <property name="orientation">vertical</property>
            <child>
              <object class="GtkBox" id="message_input_box">
                <property name="visible">True</property>
                <property name="can_focus">False</property>
                <property name="resize_mode">immediate
                </property>
                <property name="homogeneous">True</property>
                <child>
                  <object class="GtkLabel" id="message_input_bo">
                    <property name="visible">True</property>
                    <property name="can_focus">False</property>
```

```
        <property name="label" translatable="yes">
        What does the cat say:</property>

      </object>
      <packing>
        <property name="expand">False</property>
        <property name="fill">True</property>
        <property name="position">0</property>
      </packing>
    </child>
    <child>
      <object class="GtkEntry" id="message_input">
        <property name="visible">True</property>
        <property name="can_focus">True</property>
      </object>
      <packing>
        <property name="expand">False</property>
        <property name="fill">True</property>
        <property name="position">1</property>
      </packing>
    </child>
  </object>
  <packing>
    <property name="expand">False</property>
    <property name="fill">True</property>
    <property name="position">0</property>
  </packing>
</child>
<child>
  <object class="GtkBox" id="is_dead_switch_box">
    <property name="visible">True</property>
    <property name="can_focus">False</property>
```

```
<property name="homogeneous">True</property>
<child>
  <object class="GtkLabel" id="is_dead_switch_
  label">
    <property name="visible">True</property>
    <property name="can_focus">False</property>
    <property name="label" translatable="yes">
    Dead?</property>
  </object>
  <packing>
    <property name="expand">False</property>
    <property name="fill">True</property>
    <property name="position">0</property>
  </packing>
</child>
<child>
  <object class="GtkSwitch" id="is_dead_switch">
    <property name="visible">True</property>
    <property name="can_focus">True</property>
  </object>
  <packing>
    <property name="expand">False</property>
    <property name="fill">True</property>
    <property name="position">1</property>
  </packing>
</child>
</object>
<packing>
  <property name="expand">False</property>
  <property name="fill">True</property>
  <property name="position">1</property>
</packing>
```

```
    </child>
    <child>
      <object class="GtkButton" id="generate_btn">
        <property name="label" translatable="yes">
        Generate</property>
        <property name="visible">True</property>
        <property name="can_focus">True</property>
        <property name="receives_default">True</property>
      </object>
      <packing>
        <property name="expand">False</property>
        <property name="fill">True</property>
        <property name="position">2</property>
      </packing>
    </child>
  </object>
  <packing>
    <property name="expand">False</property>
    <property name="fill">True</property>
    <property name="position">0</property>
  </packing>
</child>
<child>
  <object class="GtkSeparator" id="separator1">
    <property name="visible">True</property>
    <property name="can_focus">False</property>
  </object>
  <packing>
    <property name="expand">False</property>
    <property name="fill">True</property>
    <property name="position">1</property>
  </packing>
```

```
        </child>
        <child>
          <object class="GtkBox" id="output_box">
            <property name="visible">True</property>
            <property name="can_focus">False</property>
            <property name="orientation">vertical</property>
            <child>
              <object class="GtkLabel" id="message_output">
                <property name="visible">True</property>
                <property name="can_focus">False</property>
                <property name="ellipsize">end</property>
              </object>
              <packing>
                <property name="expand">False</property>
                <property name="fill">True</property>
                <property name="position">0</property>
              </packing>
            </child>
            <child>
              <object class="GtkImage" id="image_output">
                <property name="can_focus">False</property>
                <property name="pixbuf">cat.png</property>
              </object>
              <packing>
                <property name="expand">False</property>
                <property name="fill">True</property>
                <property name="position">1</property>
              </packing>
            </child>
          </object>
```

```
        <packing>
          <property name="expand">False</property>
            <property name="fill">True</property>
            <property name="position">2</property>
        </packing>
      </child>
    </object>
  </child>
  </object>
</interface>
```

To load this XML into an actual GTK program, you need to create a new Rust project with cargo new and copy layout.glade into the src folder. Then you can open main.rs and fill in Listing 3-10. If you run the program now, you'll see Figure 3-14.

Listing 3-10. Loading the Glade XML File with GtkBuilder

```
extern crate gio;
extern crate gtk;

use gio::prelude::*;
use gtk::prelude::*;

use std::env::args;

fn build_ui(app: &gtk::Application) {
    let glade_src = include_str!("layout.glade");
    let builder = gtk::Builder::new_from_string(glade_src);

    let window: gtk::Window = builder
        .get_object("applicationwindow1").unwrap();
    window.set_application(app);

    window.show_all();
}
```

```rust
fn main() {
    let application = gtk::Application::new(
        "com.shinglyu.catsay-gui-glade",
        Default::default()
        ).expect("Failed to initialize GTK");

    application.connect_activate(|app| {
        build_ui(app);
    });

    application.run(&args().collect::<Vec<_>>());
}
```

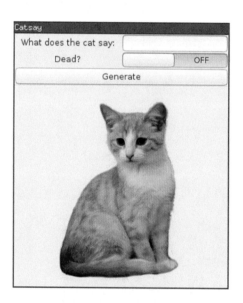

Figure 3-14. *Result of Listing 3-10*

Notice how the connect_active handler in Listing 3-10 is much simpler compared to Listing 3-7. You no longer need to build up the hierarchy inside the Rust code. Instead, you load the Glade XML file using include_str! in the build_ui() function. The built-in macro include_str!() will load a file into a string variable glade_src. You then use gtk::Builder::new_from_string(glade_src) to build the GTK program using the Glade XML definition string. However, because you are not building the widgets in Rust code, you don't have a Rust variable that points to the individual widgets, so you can't call functions like window. show_all() because window is not there.

You can identify the widgets by their IDs inside the application built by the builder. Inside Listing 3-9 the ApplicationWindow has an id="applicationwindow1" which was auto-generated by Glade. You can use builder.get object("applicationwindow1") to get the widget. Because you might provide an ID that doesn't exist, the function returns an Option<T>, so please remember to unwrap it or handle the error cases properly. The window created by the builder also doesn't know which gtk::Application it belongs to. You have to use window.set_application(app) to associate the application with the window. That's why you pass the gtk::Application created in the main function to the build_ui() function, so that the window knows which Application it should associate to.

Accepting Inputs and Button Clicks

You can add interactivity to the GTK application in a similar way you did for the TUI application. This section shows you how to add some event handlers to the inputs and buttons in the build_ui() function (see Listing 3-11).

Listing 3-11. Event Handlers for the GTK Application

```rust
fn build_ui(app: &gtk::Application) {
    let glade_src = include_str!("layout.glade");
    let builder = gtk::Builder::new_from_string(glade_src);
    let window: gtk::Window = builder
        .get_object("applicationwindow1").unwrap();
    window.set_application(app);
```

```rust
// Inputs
let message_input: gtk::Entry = builder
    .get_object("message_input").unwrap();

// Submit button
let button: gtk::Button = builder
    .get_object("generate_btn").unwrap();

// Outputs
let message_output: gtk::Label = builder
    .get_object("message_output").unwrap();
let image_output: gtk::Image = builder
    .get_object("image_output").unwrap();
let image_output_clone = image_output.clone();

button.connect_clicked(move |_| {
    message_output.set_text(&format!(
        "{}\n      \\\n        \\",
        message_input.get_text().unwrap().as_str()
    ));
    image_output_clone.show();
});

window.show_all();
image_output.hide();
}
```

First, you get the handles for all the widgets you need using the
builder.get_object() function, just like you did when getting the
ApplicationWindow:

```rust
let message_input: gtk::Entry = builder
    .get_object("message_input").unwrap();
let button: gtk::Button = builder
    .get_object("generate_btn").unwrap();
```

```
let message_output: gtk::Label = builder
    .get_object("message_output").unwrap();
let image_output: gtk::Image = builder
    .get_object("image_output").unwrap();
```

You want the cat image to remain hidden until you click the Generate button. So you call image_output.hide() right after window.show_all(). The order is important here because you first show everything then hide the image. If you hide the image first, then call widow.show_all(), the image will be shown again.

You then have to create a callback function on the Generate button to show the cat and the text message. You call button.connect_clicked() to set the callback for the button's clicked event:

```
button.connect_clicked(|_| {
    message_output.set_text(&format!(
        "{}\n      \\\n         \\",
        message_input.get_text().unwrap().as_str()
    });
    image_output.show();
));
```

The callback is a closure and it does three things:

- Reads the input from message_input.get_text(). (get_text() returns a glib::GString, so you have to convert it to &str using .as_str().)

- Sets the message_output text using the text in message_input.

- Shows the image with image_output.show().

79

Although the structure of the code looks okay, the code won't compile. You'll receive the following error when you try to compile:

```
error[E0373]: closure may outlive the current function, but it
borrows 'image_output', which
  --> src/main.rs:36:28
   |
36 |      button.connect_clicked(|_| {
   |                             ^^^ may outlive borrowed value
                                     'image_output'
...
41 |          image_output.show();
   |          ------------ 'image_output' is borrowed here
   |
note: function requires argument type to outlive "static'
  --> src/main.rs:36:5
   |
36 | /      button.connect_clicked(|_| {
37 | |          message_output.set_text(&format!(
38 | |              "{}\n       \\\n       \\",
39 | |              message_input.get_text().unwrap().as_str()
40 | |          ));
41 | |          image_output.show();
42 | |      });
   | |_____^
help: to force the closure to take ownership of `image_output`
(and any other referenced variables), use the `move` keyword
   |
36 |      button.connect_clicked(move |_| {
   |                             ^^^^^^^^
```

This is because once the callback function is set, it might get triggered anytime during the application's lifetime. But by the time the callback is triggered, the build_ui() function is probably already finished and the image_output variable has gone out of scope. To mitigate this, you have to move the ownership of the variable to the closure, so the closure can keep it alive. But if you simply add a move keyword to the closure, the image_ output variable won't be accessible after you move it into the closure, because the ownership has already moved to the closure. For example:

```
let image_output: gtk::Image = builder
    .get_object("image_output").unwrap();

button.connect_clicked(move |_| {
    // ...
    image_output.show();
});

image_output.hide(); // This will fail!
// error[E0382]: borrow of moved value: 'image_output'
```

However, because Gtk-rs is a wrapper around the C GTK library, doing a Rust clone on an Gtk-rs object only copies the pointer. So since it's not a costly deep clone of the whole data structure, you can simply clone the handle and move it into the closure[3]:

```
let image_output: gtk::Image = builder
    .get_object("image_output").unwrap();
let image_output_clone = image_output.clone(); // low-cost clone
```

---

[3]You are not cloning message_input and message_output simply because you don't need to use them after you define the callback function. If you *did* need to use them after moving them into the callback, you should clone them just like you did for image_output.

```
button.connect_clicked(move |_| {
    message_output.set_text(&format!(
        "{}\n        \\\n        \\",
        message_input.get_text().unwrap().as_str()
    });
    image_output_clone.show(); // move the clone into the
                               // closure
));

image_output.hide(); // we still keep the ownership of it
```

Reading a gtk::Switch

There is only one thing left in the Glade design, and that's the "Dead?" switch. The code change (see Listing 3-12) is pretty straightforward.

Listing 3-12. Handling Input from gtk:Switch

```
fn build_ui(app: &gtk::Application) {
    // ...
    let is_dead_switch: gtk::Switch = builder
        .get_object("is_dead_switch").unwrap();

    let image_output: gtk::Image = builder
        .get_object("image_output").unwrap();
    let image_output_clone = image_output.clone();

    button.connect_clicked(move |_| {
        // ...
        let is_dead = is_dead_switch.get_active();
        if (is_dead) {
            image_output_clone
                .set_from_file("./images/cat_dead.png")
```

```
    } else {
        image_output_clone.set_from_file("./images/cat.png")
    }
    image_output_clone.show();
});

window.show_all();
image_output.hide();
}
```

As before, you get the handle of the switch by:

```
let is_dead_switch: gtk::Switch = builder
    .get_object("is_dead_switch").unwrap();
```

Then you can check if it's activated by reading is_dead_switch.get_ active(). Based on the whether it's true or false, you can load different cat images using image_output_clone.set_from_file("path/to/file. png"). This allows you to change the image in runtime.

Finally, the end product is shown in Figures 3-15 to 3-17.

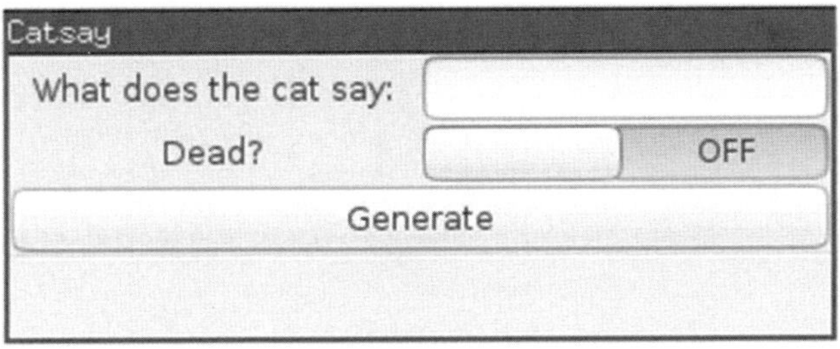

Figure 3-15. *The form*

Figure 3-16. *After clicking Generate with "Dead?" off*

Figure 3-17. *After clicking Generate with "Dead?" on*

Other Alternatives

This concludes the journey of building a text-based user interface (TUI) to a graphical user interface (GUI). I chose to use the ncurses-based TUI library and the GTK-based GUI library because they are more mature and stable. Their corresponding Rust library is also more production-ready. However, there are many exciting new Rust libraries out there that provide a more idiomatic Rust interface or provide better cross-platform support.

On the TUI side, tui-rs is a good alternative to Cursive, but it doesn't support input handling out-of-the-box, so it's better suited for building applications that don't require user interaction, like a monitoring dashboard. There are also some pure-Rust alternatives, like termion (part of ReduxOS) and crossterm. If you are looking for cross-system support, including Linux and Windows, pancurses is an abstraction layer above the platform-specific layers. It uses ncurses-rs for Linux and pdcurses-sys for Windows underneath.

On the GUI side, there are alternatives like Relm, which is also GTK based, but with an Elm-inspired API. Another very popular GUI library is Qt; there are Rust bindings for it like rust-qt and qmlrs and rute. There is also conrod, which is written entirely in Rust and is part of the Piston game engine. If you are familiar with Flutter, Google's cross-device UI toolkit, there is a Rust binding for it, called flutter-rs. Other existing GUI libraries like IUP and Dear ImGui also have their Rust bindings (iup-rust and imgui-rs, respectively).

There are many TUIs and GUIs, depending on which platform you are targeting and which library you are familiar with. There is always something to fulfill your need to build a user interface in Rust.

CHAPTER 4

Building a Game

Video games have come a long way from their early days. The Super Mario Bros for NES ran on an 8-bit CPU that had a 1.79MHz clock rate. The game itself is roughly 31KB. Nowadays, you can easily get a gaming PC that has an 8-core CPU running at 35GHz each, and games that are 50-70GB. That is thousands of times more computing power and millions of times more storage space. Games are growing more and more complex as well, so the life of a game programmer is becoming tougher than before.

Rust is potentially a great candidate for building games. Rust's low-level memory safety guarantee and exceptional performance make it ideal for building robust and performant game engines and games. At the same time, its high-level syntax allows you to write your game logic in a clean and modular way.

Although the ecosystem is still very young, there are already some beautiful games built in Rust. There are also a few game engines, which are discussed in the last section. You'll be using the Amethyst game engine to learn how to build a game in Rust. The project is still under active deployment, so the code and documentation always change rapidly. You'll be using the stable version 0.13.2.

What Are You Building?

Back in the days when Flash games were still a thing, there was a very simple but highly addictive game from Japan called "Pikachu volleyball". The game was about two Pikachus (Pokémon characters) playing beach

© Shing Lyu 2020
S. Lyu, *Practical Rust Projects*, https://doi.org/10.1007/978-1-4842-5599-5_4

volleyball. You could either play against the computer or compete with others using the same keyboard. This chapter shows you how to recreate the game (at least partially).

The game will have the following features:

- It will be a 2D game, with one player (a cat) on the left and one player on the right.

- WSAD keys control the movement of the left player, and the arrow keys control the right player.

- A ball will be fed from the middle, and each player has to bounce the ball back to the opponent using its head and body.

- The ball will bounce and fall as if there is gravity.

- You score when the ball touches the ground on the opponent's side.

- There will be music and sound effects.

Amethyst and the Entity-Component-System Pattern

Amethyst is a game engine that is built on the entity-component-system (ECS) pattern. ECS is an architectural pattern in game engine design. The core idea of ECS is to promote composition over inheritance. To give an example, imagine a role-playing game (RPG). The game has a player, some monsters, and some destructible trees. The players and monsters can move and attack, so you'll need to keep track of their location and health. When the monster touches the player, you'll need to reduce the health of the player, so you'll need to track collisions as well.

First, are *entities*. Entities are objects in the game like the player, the monsters, and the trees. Implementing all the aspects of the entities in one piece of code will quickly become unmanageable. Instead, you'll learn how to separate each aspect into *components*, and attach components onto entities, creating the game object from a collection of components. For example, you could have the following components:

- Attack: Attack power and range

- Transform: Keep track of the location

- Collision: Detect collision

- Health: Keep track of the health and death

Then the entities could be composed of:

- Player: Attack + Transform + Collision + Health

- Monster: Attack + Transform + Collision + Health

- Tree: Transform + Collision[1]

Finally, to make the game move, you'll implement *systems* to update each component. One system is responsible for one aspect of the game. For example, you could have systems like:

- Movement: Moves the entities and updates their Transform. For example, the monsters will move by themselves.

- Input: Takes user input, updates the player's location, and perform attacks.

- Collision: Checks for collisions and stop the entities from crossing each other; may also incur damage.

---

[1]You can give health to the tree, but to keep it simple, this game just assumes the tree can be destroyed with one blow.

- Attack: When an attack happens, reduces the health of the victim based on the attacker's attack power. For trees, destroys them when being attacked.

Using this architecture, you can make the code cleaner and more structured, which helps you create very complicated games.

Creating an Amethyst Project

Before you write any Amethyst code, you have to install a few dependencies for Amethyst. Amethyst relies on a few system libraries for things like sound, font rendering, XML parsing, and cryptography. Therefore, you need to install these system dependencies first. On Ubuntu,[2] you can run the following command to install them all:

```
sudo apt install gcc pkg-config openssl libasound2-dev cmake
build-essential python3 libfreetype6-dev libexpat1-dev
libxcb-composite0-dev libssl-dev
```

Back in v0.11 of Amethyst, the rendering engine[3] migrated to Rendy, a low-level rendering engine on top of gfx-hal, which is a graphics abstraction layer that can connect to different backends. On Ubuntu, you are using the Vulkan backend. Vulkan is a cross-platform 3D graphics API that is similar to the famous OpenGL. To be able to use the Vulkan backend, you also have to install a few other dependencies:

```
sudo apt-get install libvulkan-dev mesa-vulkan-drivers
vulkan-utils
```

---

[2]You can find instructions for other platforms here: https://github.com/amethyst/amethyst/blob/master/readme.md#dependencies.

[3]A rendering engine is responsible for turning the virtual world into pixels on the screen.

You'll also have to make sure you have the latest graphic card driver installed. If you use an integrated Intel HD graphics 620 GPU, it works out-of-the-box.

Then you'll need to create the project structure. In theory, you can use `cargo new` to create an empty project and add all the dependencies and code manually. However, Amethyst provides a command-line tool that saves you all the effort. First, you install the Amethyst command-line interface (CLI) with `cargo`:

```
cargo install amethyst_tools
```

Then you can create a project by running the following:

```
amethyst new cat_volleyball
```

This will create a `cat_volleyball` folder that contains a `cargo.toml` and a few template files. If you run `cargo run --features=vulkan` now you'll see an empty window being opened and a log like Listing 4-1 in the console.

Listing 4-1. Example Log Output of a New Amethyst Project

```
% cargo run --features=vulkan
    Compiling cat_volleyball v0.1.0 (/home/shinglyu/workspace/
    practical_rust/game/ cat_volleyball)
     Finished dev [unoptimized + debuginfo] target(s) in 19.13s
     Running 'target/debug/cat_volleyball'
[INFO][amethyst::app] Initializing Amethyst...
[INFO][amethyst::app] Version: 0.13.2
[INFO][amethyst::app] Platform: x86_64-unknown-linux-gnu
[INFO][amethyst::app] Amethyst git commit:
[INFO][amethyst::app] Rustc version: 1.39.0 Stable
[INFO][amethyst::app] Rustc git commit:
4560ea788cb760f0a34127156c78e2552949f734
```

```
[INFO][winit::platform::platform::x11::window] Guessed window
DPI factor: 1.75
[INFO][rendy_util::wrap] Slow safety checks are enabled! You
can disable them in production by enabling the 'no-slow-safety-
checks' feature!
[INFO][amethyst::app] Engine is shutting down
```

Creating a Window

If you open the Cargo.toml, you'll see Listing 4-2.

Listing 4-2. Cargo.toml Created by Amethyst CLI

```
[package]
name = "cat_volleyball"
version = "0.1.0"
authors = ["Shing Lyu"]
edition = "2018"

[dependencies]
amethyst = "0.13.2"

[features]
empty = ["amethyst/empty"]
metal = ["amethyst/metal"]
vulkan = ["amethyst/vulkan"]
```

Notice that the dependency amethyst = "0.13.2" is included. You also have the three possible backends in the [features] section. Since you are always using the Vulkan backend in this example, you can hard-code it in the dependencies, as shown in Listing 4-3.

Listing 4-3. Hard-Coding the Vulkan Backend

```
[package]
// ...

[dependencies]
amethyst = { version = "0.13.2", features = ["vulkan"] }
```

In `src/main.rs` (see Listing 4-4), there is quite a lot of boilerplate code for rendering a window.

Listing 4-4. Generated src/main.rs from Amethyst CLI

```rust
use amethyst::{
    core::transform::TransformBundle,
    ecs::prelude::{ReadExpect, Resource, SystemData},
    prelude::*,
    renderer::{
        plugins::{RenderFlat2D, RenderToWindow},
        types::DefaultBackend,
        RenderingBundle,
    },
    utils::application_root_dir,
};

struct MyState;

impl SimpleState for MyState {
    fn on_start(
        &mut self,
        _data: StateData<'_, GameData<'_, '_>>
    ) {}
}

fn main() -> amethyst::Result<()> {
    amethyst::start_logger(Default::default());
```

```
    let app_root = application_root_dir()?;

    let config_dir = app_root.join("config");
    let display_config_path = config_dir.join("display_config.ron");
    let assets_dir = app_root.join("assets");

    let game_data = GameDataBuilder::default()
        .with_bundle(
            RenderingBundle::<DefaultBackend>::new()
                .with_plugin(
                    RenderToWindow::from_config_path(
                        display_config_path
                    ).with_clear([0.0, 0.0, 0.0, 1.0]),
                )
                .with_plugin(RenderFlat2D::default()),
        )?
        .with_bundle(TransformBundle::new())?;

    let mut game = Application::new(assets_dir, MyState, game_data)?;
    game.run();

    Ok(())
}
```

Let's first take a look at the high-level structure of the game. Similar to the GUI program in the previous chapter, you initialize an Application and call .run() on it near the end of the main() function. The Application constructor takes three things to initialize: assets_dir, MyState, and game_data. The first parameter assets_dir is pretty self-explanatory; it points to the directory that contains all the assets, like configuration files, images, textures, and audio. You don't want to hard-code the path, so you should use the following code to get the relative path to the assets folder under the project's root directory

```
let app_root = application_root_dir()?;
let assets_dir = app_root.join("assets");
```

The second argument, called MyState, is a struct defined before the main() function. It implements the SimpleState trait. A "state" in Amethyst's term is a global game state. For example, when the cat volleyball game starts up, it enters a loading screen. You can create a LoadingState for it. Once the game is loaded, players enter a character selection screen where they can choose different cat avatars. This can be implemented in a CharacterSelectionState. After the users select their character, the game starts, entering the GameplayState. If you allow the user to enter the pause menu with the ESC key, you can add a transition from GameplayState to a PauseState.

Adding these states makes it easy for the developer to separate the concerns for a different state of the game and make the game's flow easier to reason about. Amethyst provides a built-in state manager, which uses a pushdown-automaton concept to control the transition between states. However, to keep this example game simple, you are going to use only one state. By implementing the SimpleState trait on the MyState struct, you declare it a state so the state manager can use it. SimpleState also implements the logic to cleanly quit the game engine when you close the window.

The last argument, game_data, is how you tell the game engine to load everything you need. The game_data is built up by the GameDataBuilder, by which you attach all the prebuilt modules/components you need to make the game work. To make the code less verbose, Amethyst groups many related pieces of code into "bundles". For example, in Listing 4-4, RenderingBundle and TransformBundle are added to GameDataBuilder.

The TransformBundle will register the transform components and the transform system to the game engine so that you can start assigning the location of game entities and move them around. The RenderingBundle is a special bundle, and it has a plugin system that you can use to mix plugins to create the bundle that meets your needs.

The first plugin you add is RenderToWindow, which creates a window for you. It takes a display_config_path, which points to the display_config.ron file in the resource directory (see Listing 4-5).

Listing 4-5. Displaying config.ron

```
(
  title: "cat_volleyball",
  dimensions: Some((500, 500)),
)
```

The display_config.ron file contains configurations about the window. For example, dimensions = some((500, 500)) sets the window size to 500×500 pixels.

You also call .with_clear() function on the RenderToWindow plugin. The parameters are RGBA values, so (0.0, 0.0, 0.0, 1.0) mean solid black. This will render a window with a solid black background.

You then add the RenderFlat2D plugin. This adds all the things required for rendering a 2D game. It also implicitly adds a spritesheet processor, which gives you the ability to draw 2D objects from a big texture picture. I explain the concept of a spritesheet in the section entitled "Adding the Cats".

Once you have the boilerplate code and the rendering pipeline ready, you can open an empty window with cargo run (see Figure 4-1).

Figure 4-1. *Opening an empty screen*

Seeing the World Through a Camera

To make the code cleaner, you are going to move the only game state into another file, called `src/catvolleyball.rs` (see Listing 4-6).

Listing 4-6. Moving the Game State to a Separate File

```
use amethyst::{core::transform::Transform, prelude::*,
    renderer::Camera};

pub const ARENA_HEIGHT: f32 = 500.0;
pub const ARENA_WIDTH: f32 = 500.0;

pub struct CatVolleyball;

impl SimpleState for CatVolleyball {}
```

You rename the state to `CatVolleyball` and define some constants for the game arena's width and height, which you'll be using shortly.

Although the game engine will create a virtual world, it doesn't know which part of the world to display on the screen. Therefore, you need to create a camera that tells the engine which part of the engine should be displayed and from which angle. You can add a function to set up this camera in the src/catvolleyball.rs file, as shown in Listing 4-7.

Listing 4-7. Initializing the Camera

```
use amethyst::{core::transform::Transform, prelude::*,
    renderer::Camera};

fn initialize_camera(world: &mut World) {
    let mut transform = Transform::default();
    transform.set_translation_xyz(
        ARENA_WIDTH * 0.5,
        ARENA_HEIGHT * 0.5,
        1.0
    );
    world
        .create_entity()
        .with(Camera::standard_2d(ARENA_WIDTH, ARENA_HEIGHT))
        .with(transform)
        .build();
}

pub struct CatVolleyball;

impl SimpleState for CatVolleyball {
    fn on_start(&mut self, data: StateData<'_, GameData<'_, '_>>) {
        let world = data.world;

        initialize_camera(world);
    }
}
```

In the initialize_camera() function, you create a camera entity in the world using world.create_entity(). You set the camera to be Camera::standard_2d(ARENA_WIDTH, ARENA_HEIGHT). This will create an orthographic projection[4] camera that covers an area of ARENA_WIDTH by ARENA_HEIGHT. You move the camera to the center of the arena with transform. This transform is a translation of X = half the arena width, Y = half the arena height and Z = 1, as shown in Figure 4-2.

When should you run the initialize_camera() function? Each state in Amethyst has a few lifetime events, like start, stop, pause, resume, etc. Since there is only one state in the game, it makes sense to initialize the camera in the start event of the main state. That's why you add the initialize_camera(world) call to the on_start() function in CatVolleyball State. Notice that you pass the world to the initialize_camera() call so you can add the camera to it. The World is basically a holder for Resources and some helper function to help you retrieve or update the Resources. Resources are data structures that hold data needed across the game, but not specific to any entity. For example, the camera or the score of the game should be created as Resources. You pass the World to the on_start() function as a parameter, wrapped inside the StateData.

---

[4]Orthographic projection will make the game appear "flat," as opposed to perspective projection. It is commonly used in 2D games.

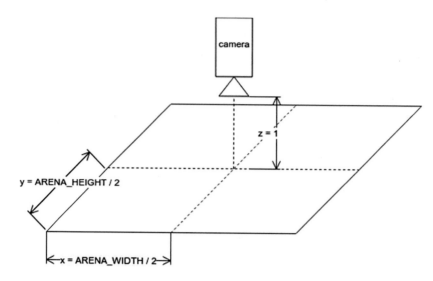

Figure 4-2. *Camera location*

Adding the Cats

Finally, you are going to add some moving parts to the game. First, you need to add the two cat players to the game. Add the code in Listing 4-8 to src/catvolleyball.rs.

Listing 4-8. The Player Entity

```
pub const PLAYER_HEIGHT: f32 = 32.0;
pub const PLAYER_WIDTH: f32 = 22.0;

#[derive(PartialEq, Eq)]
pub enum Side {
    Left,
    Right,
}
```

```rust
pub struct Player {
    pub side: Side,
    pub width: f32,
    pub height: f32,
}

impl Player {
    fn new(side:Side) -> Player {
        Player {
            side,
            width: PLAYER_WIDTH,
            height: PLAYER_HEIGHT,
        }
    }
}

impl Component for Player {
    type Storage = DenseVecStorage<Self>;
}
```

The Player struct is pretty simple. It has a width and height and a
Side enum. The Side enum is used to identify which side the user is on.
The type Storage = DenseVecStorage<Self> line tells the game engine
how to store the component in memory. There are many storage types, but
the DenseVecStorage you choose will store the component in a contiguous
vector. This is ideal for small components that are carried by most entities
because it uses less memory.

Next, you need to initialize the players in the world as you did for the
camera (see Listing 4-9).

Listing 4-9. Initializing the Players

```
fn initialize_players(world: &mut World) {
    let mut left_transform = Transform::default();
    let mut right_transform = Transform::default();

    let y = PLAYER_HEIGHT / 2.0;
    left_transform.set_translation_xyz(PLAYER_WIDTH * 0.5, y, 0.0);
    right_transform.set_translation_xyz(ARENA_WIDTH -
    PLAYER_WIDTH * 0.5, y, 0.0);

    world
        .create_entity()
        .with(Player::new(Side::Left))
        .with(left_transform)
        .build();

    world
        .create_entity()
        .with(Player::new(Side::Right))
        .with(right_transform)
        .build();
}

impl SimpleState for CatVolleyball {
    fn on_start(&mut self, data: StateData<'_, GameData<'_, '_>>) {
        let world = data.world;

        initialize_camera(world);
        world.register::<Player>();
        initialize_players(world);
}
```

In the code, you first set up the location of the two players using
`Transform::set_translation_xyz()`. You place the players on each
side of the arena, as shown in Figures 4-3 and 4-4. Then you create the
two `Player` entities in the `World`, one with `Side::Left` and one with
`Side::Right`.

Just like the camera, this `initialize_players()` function is executed
in the `CatVolleyball` state's `on_start()` event handler. Usually, when
you use a component in a system, it will be automatically registered in
the `World`, and its `Storage` will be initialized. But since you don't have a
system yet, you have to manually register the components using `world.`
`register::<Player>()`.

So far, you have defined the internal data structure of the `Player`, but
you haven't defined how the `Players` look. You need to have an image of
the cat `Players` and ask the game engine to draw the players using that
image. Using an individual image for each thing on the screen is typically
too inefficient for a game, because the image (texture) needs to be loaded
onto the GPU, which has a high overhead. Instead, you should aggregate
all the images (or some of the related ones) into a big picture called the
spritesheet. Then you "cut out" a small section of the big image for each
item. This way, you reduce the overall loading time and allow the GPU to
handle the images more efficiently.

Now, because the cat player is the only sprite there is so far, you use
a single cat image as the spritesheet. Draw a cat in pixel art style (see
Figure 4-5) and save it as `assets/texture.spritesheet.png`.

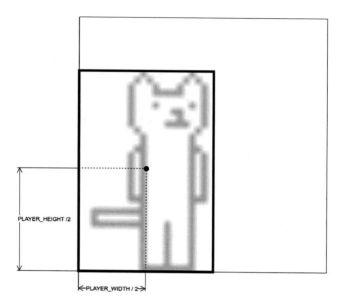

Figure 4-3. *Left player location*

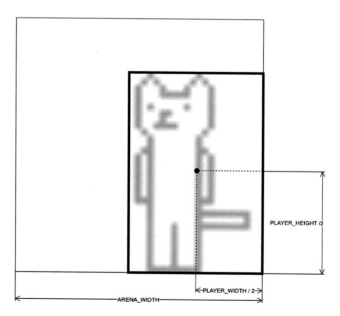

Figure 4-4. *Right player location*

Figure 4-5. *spritesheet.png*

Usually, the spritesheet contains more than one image; you need to provide the coordinates for each image inside the spritesheet so that Amethyst knows how to split it. You'll write the coordinates in the `assets/texture/spritesheet.ron` file (see Listing 4-10). It specifies the total width and height of the spritesheet, and a list of positions and dimensions of the individual images (i.e., sprites).

Listing 4-10. Spritesheet Definition

```
(
    texture_width: 22,
    texture_height: 32,
    sprites: [
        (
            x: 0,
            y: 0,
            width: 22,
            height: 32,
        ),
    ],
)
```

In older versions of Amethyst, you needed to add a spritesheet processor to the `GameDataBuilder` so that the spritesheet could take effect, but now the `RenderFlat2D` plugin in the `RenderingBundle` will add the spritesheet processor for you.

Then in `src/catvolleyball.rs`, you add a new functions to load them (see Listing 4-11).

Listing 4-11. Loading the Spritesheet

```
use amethyst::{
    assets::{AssetStorage, Handle, Loader},
    renderer::{Camera, ImageFormat, SpriteRender, SpriteSheet,
        SpriteSheetFormat, Texture},
};

fn load_sprite_sheet(world: &mut World) -> Handle<SpriteSheet> {
    let texture_handle = {
        let loader = world.read_resource::<Loader>();
        let texture_storage = world
            .read_resource::<AssetStorage<Texture>>();
        loader.load(
            "texture/spritesheet.png",
            ImageFormat::default(),
            (),
            &texture_storage,
        )
    };
    let loader = world.read_resource::<Loader>();
    let sprite_sheet_store = world
        .read_resource::<AssetStorage<SpriteSheet>>();
    loader.load(
        "texture/spritesheet.ron",
        SpriteSheetFormat(texture_handle),
        (),
        &sprite_sheet_store,
    )
}
```

```
pub struct CatVolleyball;
impl SimpleState for CatVolleyball {
    fn on_start(&mut self, data: StateData<'_, GameData<'_, '_>>) {
        let world = data.world;
        let sprite_sheet_handle = load_sprite_sheet(world);

        initialize_players(world,  sprite_sheet_handle);

        // ...
    }
}
```

A piece of resource, like a spritesheet, might be used by many
different entities in a game. Therefore, loading a copy for every entity
is inefficient. Amethyst puts the resource in a reference called Handle,
which can easily be shared without deep copying the memory. That's
why the load_sprite_sheet() function returns a Handle<SpriteSheet>
instead of the SpriteSheet itself. In the load_sprite_sheet() function,
you first load the png texture into an AssetStorage<Texture>, using the
loader.load() provided by the World. The AssetStorage is a centralized
place for the World to store the resource for optimal efficiency. The call
to loader.load() returns a Handle to the texture. This texture handle
is then passed to another loader that will load the spritesheet.ron.
One thing to keep in mind is that these loaders load the resources
asynchronously, so they might not be immediately available after calling
loader.load().

Finally, you load the spritesheet in the CatVolleyball state's on_
start() handler and pass it to the initialize_players() function as a
second parameter, as shown in Listing 4-12.

Listing 4-12. Initializing the Players with the Spritesheet

```
use amethyst::renderer::{SpriteRender, SpriteSheet,
    SpriteSheetFormat, Texture},

fn initialize_players(
    world: &mut World,
    sprite_sheet: Handle // Extra parameter
) {

    // preparing left_transform and right_transform

    let sprite_render = SpriteRender {
        sprite_sheet: sprite_sheet.clone(),
        sprite_number: 0, // cat is the first sprite in the
        sprites list
    };
    world
        .create_entity()
        .with(sprite_render.clone()) // With the sprite renderer
        .with(Player::new(Side::Left))
        .with(left_transform)
        .build();

    world
        .create_entity()
        .with(sprite_render.clone())
        .with(Player::new(Side::Right))
        .with(right_transform)
        .build();
}
```

You create the SpriteRender and tell it to render the sprite with index 0 in the list, which happens to be the only sprite in the spritesheet. Then you attach the SpriteRender to the left and right players when you create the entities. Once you run `cargo run`, you can finally see something other than a black screen (see Figure 4-6).

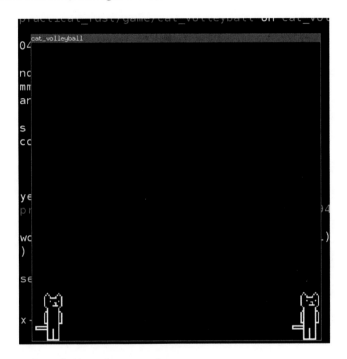

Figure 4-6. *Rendering the cat players*

Moving the Cats

The cats are now rendered nicely, but they are static. You want to control them with a keyboard. To avoid hardcoding all they key mappings in the code, you'll can use a configuration file to define how the keys map to the actions. Let's create an input configuration file called `resources/ bindings_config.rs` like the one shown in Listing 4-13.

Listing 4-13. resources/bindings_config.rs

```
(
    axes: {
      "left_player": Emulated(pos: Key(D), neg: Key(A)),
       "right_player": Emulated(pos: Key(Right), neg: Key(Left)),
    },
    actions: {},
)
```

You register two axes: the left player is controlled by WSAD keys common in first-person shooter games, and the right player is controlled by the arrow keys. To load this configuration into the game, you need to add the InputBundle to your GameData in src/main.rs (see Listing 4-14).

Listing 4-14. Adding the InputBundle

```
use amethyst::input::{InputBundle, StringBindings},

fn main() -> amethyst::Result<()> {
    // ...
    let binding_path = app_root.join("resources")
        .join("bindings_config.ron");
    let input_bundle = InputBundle::<StringBindings>::new()
        .with_bindings_from_file(binding_path)?;

    let game_data = GameDataBuilder::default()
        // ... other bundles
        .with_bundle(input_bundle)?
}
```

Amethyst now listens to keypresses, thanks to the InputBundle, but you still need to define how to respond to those keypresses. You are going to introduce your first system for this task. First, create a Rust module in src/systems/mod.rs (see Listing 4-15). This module will contain all the systems you are going to add to the game.

Listing 4-15. The systems Module

```
mod player;

pub use self::player::PlayerSystem;
```

Then you can create the PlayerSystem in src/systems/players.rs, as shown in Listing 4-16.

Listing 4-16. The PlayerSystem Definition

```
use amethyst::::{
    core::Transform,
    core::SystemDesc,
    derive::SystemDesc,
    ecs::{Join, Read, ReadStorage, System, SystemData, World,
        WriteStorage},
    input::{InputHandler, StringBindings},
};

use crate::catvolleyball::{Player, Side, ARENA_WIDTH,
    PLAYER_WIDTH};

#[derive(SystemDesc)]
pub struct PlayerSystem;

impl<'s> System<'s> for PlayerSystem {
    type SystemData = (
        WriteStorage<'s, Transform>,
        ReadStorage<'s, Player>,
        Read<'s, InputHandler<StringBindings>>,
    );
```

```rust
fn run(
    &mut self,
    (mut transforms, players, input): Self::SystemData
) {
    for (player, transform) in
        (&players, &mut transforms).join() {
        let movement = match player.side {
            Side::Left => input.axis_value("left_player"),
            Side::Right => input.axis_value("right_player"),
        };

        if let Some(mv_amount) = movement {
            if mv_amount != 0.0 {
                let side_name = match player.side {
                    Side::Left => "left",
                    Side::Right => "right",
                };
                println!(
                    "Side {:?} moving {}",
                    side_name, mv_amount
                );
            }
        }
    }
}
```

A *system* is a struct implementing the System<'s> trait. Because you don't want to load all the resources, components, and entities in every system, a system has to say which resources/component/entity it needs explicitly. The system specifies the SystemData associate type in the

System<'s> trait to enumerate the things it needs. In PlayerSystem, you use a few different helper types in the SystemData to get the data you want:

- Read<'a, Resource>: Get an immutable reference to the Resource. You use this to get the InputHandler.

- ReadStorage<'a, Component>: Get an immutable reference to the entire storage of the Component type. You use this to get the Players.

- WriteStorage<'a, Component>: Get a mutable reference to the entire storage of the Component type. You use this to get the Transform. You use the mutable reference because eventually you'll be modifying the transform (i.e. the location of the players).

There are other types, like Write, ReadExpect, WriteExpect, Entities, etc. You can find out more about them in the Amethyst book's "System" chapter[5].

When the game engine starts running, a *dispatcher* in the game engine tries to execute the systems repeatedly. However, different systems may use the same shared resources. The dispatcher is responsible for coordinating the execution of the systems to avoid a data race, but also maximize parallelism as much as possible.

When the dispatcher decides it's time to execute PlayerSystem, it will call the run() function and pass the SystemData as the parameter. You expand the SystemData in the parameter to transform, players, and input so you can use them separately. For each player, you read the movement amount using input.axis_value(). This movement is an Option; if the key is pressed, it will be Some(mv_amount), with mv_amount being the movement amount. You now simply print the amount out for a quick test.

---

[5]https://book.amethyst.rs/stable/concepts/system.html?highlight=Read
Expect#accessing-the-context-of-the-game

Soon you'll change it to actually move the players on screen. If you type
cargo run and try to press A, D, left arrow, or right arrow, you'll see the
lines like "Side left moving …" in the log.

You also derived the SystemDesc trait on the PlayerSystem. Some
systems might need to access resources in the World during initialization.
You need to define how to get the required resource from the World
and initialize the system inside the SystemDesc implementation.
Therefore, instead of directly initializing each system and passing it
to the GameDataBuilder, you pass the SystemDesc for the systems.
The GameDataBuilder will defer these system-initialization processes
after the World is created. For systems that don't need special things
from the World, you can use the automatic derive of SystemDesc to
create a default implementation. Listing 4-16 uses core::SystemDesc,
derive::SystemDesc, also it's implicitly required to use esc::SystemData
and esc::World.

Once you are sure the input handler works, you can start implementing
the movement logic in PlayerSystem (see Listing 4-17).

Listing 4-17. Moving the Players with the PlayerSystem

```rust
// ...

const PLAYER_SPEED: f32 = 60.0;
#[derive(SystemDesc)]
pub struct PlayerSystem;

impl<'s> System<'s> for PlayerSystem {
    type SystemData = (
        WriteStorage<'s, Transform>,
        ReadStorage<'s, Player>,
        Read<'s, Time>, // We need to read the time difference
        Read<'s, InputHandler<StringBindings>>,
    );
```

114

```rust
fn run(
    &mut self,
    (mut transforms, players, time, input): Self::SystemData
) {
    for (player, transform) in
        (&players, &mut transforms).join() {
        let movement = match player.side {
            Side::Left => input.axis_value("left_player"),
            Side::Right => input.axis_value("right_player"),
        };
        if let Some(mv_amount) = movement {
            let scaled_amount = (
                PLAYER_SPEED *
                time.delta_seconds() *
                mv_amount
            ) as f32;
            let player_x = transform.translation().x;
            let player_left_limit = match player.side {
                Side::Left => 0.0,
                Side::Right => ARENA_WIDTH / 2.0,
            };
            transform.set_translation_x(
                (player_x + scaled_amount)
                    .max(player_left_limit + PLAYER_WIDTH / 2.0)
                    .min(
                        player_left_limit +
                        ARENA_WIDTH / 2.0 -
                        PLAYER_WIDTH / 2.0
                    ),
            );
        }
```

```
        }
    }
}
```

You read the mv_amount as before, but this time, you use the mv_amount to determine how to move the player. To let the players move smoothly, you set a fixed speed in PLAYER_SPEED. The time difference between two executions of the system can be read from time.delta_seconds(). This is why you also include Read<'s, Time> in the SystemData. The offset by which the user should move is thus

$$offset = player\ speed \times time\ delta \times movement\ amount$$

which corresponds to the line:

```
let scaled_amount = (
    PLAYER_SPEED *
    time.delta_seconds() *
    mv_amount
) as f32;
```

Once the offset is calculated, you can update the player's X position as so:

$$x_{after} = x_{before} + offset$$

You can get the current position (x_{before}) using let player_x = transform.translation().x;. So the final position is simply player_x + scaled_amount.

However, if you don't restrict the range of player_x, players can move out of the window and into each other's fields. Therefore, you have to limit the player_x value to only half of the arena. The left player's range will be [0, arena_width / 2] and the right player will be [arena_width / 2, arena_width]. You can easily say that the *left limit* is 0 for the left player and arena_width / 2 for the right player. Then the *right limit* is simply *left limit* + *arena width/2*. So to limit the range of *player_x*, you use the maximum and minimum function:

$$min\big(max\big(player\_x,\ left\_limit\big),\ right\_limit\big)$$

You also subtract half of the player's width from each side, because its center point locates the player. If you don't consider the player's width, the player can have half of its body outside of the arena or on the opponent's side. Figure 4-7 shows moving the cat players with the keyboard.

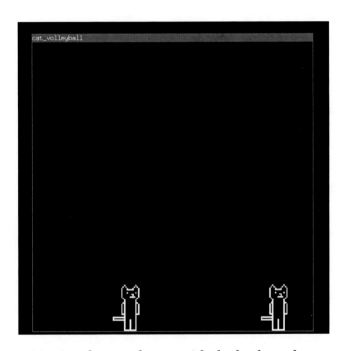

Figure 4-7. *Moving the cat players with the keyboard*

Creating the Ball

Now that you have the players ready, it's time to bring the ball into the game. Adding a Ball component is as straightforward as adding the Players. In the src/catvolleyball.rs file, you add the struct, implement

117

the Component trait on it, and add a function in the on_start method in the main state (see Listing 4-18).

Listing 4-18. Creating the Ball Component and Initializing It

```
pub const BALL_VELOCITY_X: f32 = 30.0;
pub const BALL_VELOCITY_Y: f32 = 0.0;
pub const BALL_RADIUS: f32 = 4.0;

pub struct Ball {
    pub velocity: [f32; 2],
    pub radius: f32,
}

impl Component for Ball {
    type Storage = DenseVecStorage<Self>;
}

/// Initializes one ball in the middle-ish of the arena.
fn initialize_ball(
    world: &mut World,
    sprite_sheet_handle: Handle<SpriteSheet>
) {
    // Create the translation.
    let mut local_transform = Transform::default();
    local_transform.set_translation_xyz(
        ARENA_WIDTH / 2.0, ARENA_HEIGHT / 2.0, 0.0
    );

    // Assign the sprite for the ball
    let sprite_render = SpriteRender {
        sprite_sheet: sprite_sheet_handle,
        sprite_number: 2, // ball is the third sprite on the
                          // spritesheet
    };
```

```
    world
        .create_entity()
        .with(sprite_render)
        .with(Ball {
            radius: BALL_RADIUS,
            velocity: [BALL_VELOCITY_X, BALL_VELOCITY_Y],
        })
        .with(local_transform)
        .build();
}

pub struct CatVolleyball;

impl SimpleState for CatVolleyball {
    fn on_start(&mut self, data: StateData<'_, GameData<'_, '_>>) {
        // ...
        initialize_ball(world, sprite_sheet_handle.clone());
        // ...
    }
}
```

You first define some constants like the initial velocity and the radius of the ball. Then you create the Ball struct, which contains the velocity and radius. You turn the Ball into a Component by implementing the Component trait on it. Then you build the function to initialize the ball. First, you place the ball in the center of the area using set_translation_xyz(). You also specify its sprite, which I'll cover later. Then you create the entity in the world as before.

Since you need an image for the ball, you need to add a sprite to the spritesheet. Another cat sprite is also added at this point that faces a different direction, so the cats on each side face each other. The spritesheet looks like Figure 4-8. The spritesheet.ron needs to be updated to include the new sprites (see Listing 4-19). Listing 4-18 states that the sprite for the ball has an index 2, which is the third element in the list. Once all the sprites are in place, the game will look like Figure 4-9.

Figure 4-8. *Updated spritesheet.png*

Listing 4-19. Updated spritesheet.ron

```
(
    texture_width: 58,
    texture_height: 34,
    sprites: [
        (
            x: 11,
            y: 1,
            width: 22,
            height: 32,
        ),
        (
            x: 35,
            y: 1,
            width: 22,
            height: 32,
        ),
        (
            x: 1,
            y: 1,
            width: 8,
            height: 8,
        ),
    ],
)
```

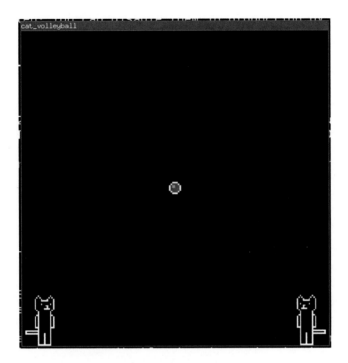

Figure 4-9. *Game with updated sprites*

Can't Defy Gravity

In the previous section, you gave the ball an initial velocity that goes toward the right. However, the ball flies toward the right and out of the window as if it's in zero gravity. You need to implement a system that simulates gravity. Adding the code skeleton for the system is simple: add a `src/systems/move_balls.rs` file and paste the code shown in Listing 4-20 into it.

Listing 4-20. Ball Movement System

```
use amethyst::{
    core::timing::Time,
    core::transform::Transform,
    core::SystemDesc,
```

```
    derive::SystemDesc,
    ecs::prelude::{Join, Read, System, SystemData, World,
        WriteStorage}
};

use crate::catvolleyball::Ball;

#[derive(SystemDesc)]
pub struct MoveBallsSystem;

pub const GRAVITY_ACCELERATION: f32 = -40.0;

impl<'s> System<'s> for MoveBallsSystem {
    type SystemData = (
        WriteStorage<'s, Ball>,
        WriteStorage<'s, Transform>,
        Read<'s, Time>,
    );

    fn run(
        &mut self,
        (mut balls, mut locals, time): Self::SystemData
    ) {
        // Move every ball according to its speed, and the time
        // passed.
        // https://gamedev.stackexchange.com/questions/15708/
        // how-can-i-implement-gravity.
        for (ball, local) in (&mut balls, &mut locals).join() {
            local.prepend_translation_x(
                ball.velocity[0] * time.delta_seconds()
            );
```

```
        local.prepend_translation_y(
            (
                ball.velocity[1] +
                time.delta_seconds() *
                GRAVITY_ACCELERATION / 2.0
            ) * time.delta_seconds(),
        );
        ball.velocity[1] = ball.velocity[1] +
            time.delta_seconds() * GRAVITY_ACCELERATION;
        }
    }
}
```

This system takes three SystemData: the ball (for getting and updating its velocity), the transform (for moving the ball), and the time (to know the time difference between executions). Based on the definition of acceleration:

$$x(t) = \frac{d}{dx}v(t)$$
$$v(t) = \frac{d}{dx}y(t)$$

It might be tempting to write:

```
velocity = velocity + acceleration * time_difference
y = y + velocity * time_difference
```

However, this approach (known as *Euler integration*) introduces some error that is dependent on the time difference, and it is noticeable when the time difference is not steady. If the frame rate is different, the trajectory of the ball will also be slightly different. To fix the issue, you can use a different algorithm called *velocity Verlet integration*:

```
y = y + (velocity + time_difference * acceleration / 2) *
  time_difference
velocity = velocity + acceleration * time_difference
```

This gives a much more accurate simulation of a falling ball. You also advance the x position of the ball by x_velocity + time_difference, because this axis is not affected by gravity.

Once the system is ready, you can expose it in src/systems/mod.rs:

```
mod move_balls;

pub use self::move_balls::MoveBallsSystem;
```

Then you can use this system by adding it to the GameData in src/main.rs (see Listing 4-21).

Listing 4-21. Using the MoveBallSystem

```
// ...

fn main() -> amethyst::Result<()> {
    // ...
    let game_data = GameDataBuilder::default()
        // ...
        .with(systems::MoveBallsSystem, "ball_system", &[])
        // ...
}
```

Now, if you run cargo run, the ball shoots to the right and falls in a beautiful curve.

Making the Ball Bounce

The ball now drops naturally, but it falls through the floor and the cat players. To make the game playable, you need to implement the bounce system that makes the ball bounce when it hits the boundary of the window or the player. This is as simple as adding another system to the game (see Listing 4-22). One subtle difference is that you have to define the dependencies in the call to GameDataBuilder::default().with(). The third parameter in that call is a list of systems that must be fully running before this one (the BounceSystem) can run. Because you need the players and the ball all to be ready, so you can handle the bounce behavior between them, you let the BounceSystem wait for the other two.

Listing 4-22. Bounce System Skeleton

```
// src/systems/mod.rs
// ...
mod bounce;
pub use self::bounce::BounceSystem;

// src/main.rs
// ...
fn main() -> amethyst::Result<()> {
    // ...
    let game_data = GameDataBuilder::default()
        // ...
        .with(
            systems::BounceSystem,
            "collision_system",
            &["player_system", "ball_system"], // dependencies
        )
        // ...
}
```

```
// src/systems/bounce.rs
// ...
#[derive(SystemDesc)]
pub struct BounceSystem;

impl<'s> System<'s> for BounceSystem {
    // ...
}
```

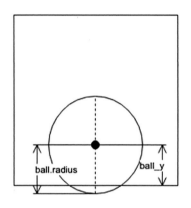

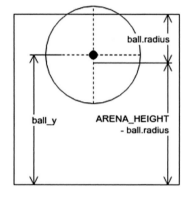

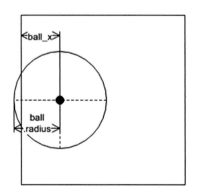

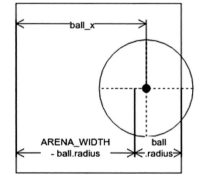

Figure 4-10. *Bouncing at the edge*

First, you'll learn to handle the bouncing around the edge of the window. In each frame, you track the location of the ball; if the ball has gone outside of any edge, and its velocity is making the ball going out even farther[6], then you'll invert the velocity on that axis. For example, if the ball goes outside of the right edge, and its x velocity is +10 pixel/sec (i.e., moving toward the right), then you flip the x velocity to -10 pixel/sec (i.e., moving toward the left). Generalize this idea to the four edges and you get Listing 4-23. The four cases in Listing 4-23 are illustrated in Figure 4-10.

Listing 4-23. Bouncing the Ball at the Edge

```
use amethyst::{
    core::transform::Transform,
    core::SystemDesc,
    derive::SystemDesc,
    ecs::prelude::{Join, Read, ReadExpect, ReadStorage,
        System, SystemData, World, WriteStorage},
};

use crate::catvolleyball::{Ball, Player, Side, ARENA_HEIGHT,
    ARENA_WIDTH};

#[derive(SystemDesc)]
pub struct BounceSystem;

impl<'s> System<'s> for BounceSystem {
    type SystemData = (
        WriteStorage<'s, Ball>,
        ReadStorage<'s, Player>,
        ReadStorage<'s, Transform>,
    );
```

---

[6]This is required because sometimes the ball already bounced, but it's still outside of the window in the next frame. In this case, the ball will be trapped at the edge because the velocity keeps inverting.

```
fn run(&mut self, (mut balls, players, transforms):
    Self::SystemData) {
    /* Check whether a ball collided, and bounce off
       accordingly.
       We also check for the velocity of the ball every
       time, to prevent multiple collisions
       from occurring. */
    for (ball, transform) in (&mut balls, &transforms).join() {
        let ball_x = transform.translation().x;
        let ball_y = transform.translation().y;

        // Bounce at the four sides of the arena.
        if ball_y <= ball.radius && ball.velocity[1] < 0.0 {
            ball.velocity[1] = -ball.velocity[1];
        } else if ball_y >= (ARENA_HEIGHT - ball.radius)
            && ball.velocity[1] > 0.0 {
            ball.velocity[1] = -ball.velocity[1];
        } else if ball_x <= (ball.radius)
            && ball.velocity[0] < 0.0 {
            ball.velocity[0] = -ball.velocity[0];
        } else if ball_x >= (ARENA_WIDTH - ball.radius)
            && ball.velocity[0] > 0.0 {
            ball.velocity[0] = -ball.velocity[0];
        }
    }
    }
}
```

You also need to make the ball bounce when it hits the players. Otherwise, it passes through the players as if they are thin air. You don't need to define the contour of the player and do a real physical collision simulation. You can simplify this by imagining the player to be a rectangular box, and if the ball's location falls in this box, you assume that the ball collides with the player (see Figure 4-11). You can put this collision logic in a helper function and put it in src/systems/bounce.rs (see Listing 4-24).

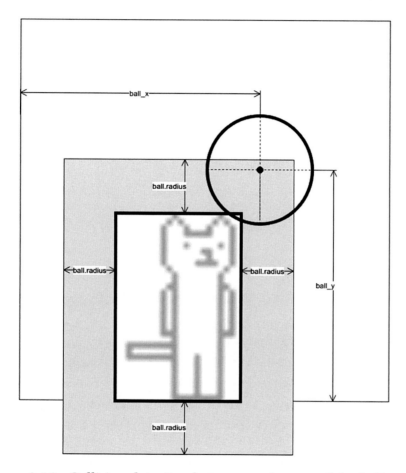

Figure 4-11. *Collision detection between a player and the ball*

Listing 4-24. Utility Function for Determining Ball Collision with the Player

```
// A point is in a box when its coordinates are smaller or
// equal than the top right and larger or equal than
// the bottom left.
fn point_in_rect(
    x: f32, // ball's x and y location
    y: f32,
    left: f32, // the player box's boundary
    bottom: f32,
    right: f32,
    top: f32
) -> bool {
    x >= left && x <= right && y >= bottom && y <= top
}
```

When it collides, you don't calculate the direction it should bounce back according to physics. Instead, you invert the Y-axis velocity, so the falling ball now bounces upward. For the X-axis, you force the ball to fly toward the opponent. So for the left player, the ball will go right when hit, and vice versa. To give the game some playability, you can randomly speed up or slow down the ball in the X-axis on collision, so the ball's trajectory is unpredictable. You can use these rules to make the calculation simple but keep the game interesting. The code for this algorithm is shown in Listing 4-25.

Listing 4-25. Bouncing the Ball Upon Collision with Players

```
// ...
extern crate rand;
use rand::Rng;

// ...
```

```rust
impl<'s> System<'s> for BounceSystem {
    // ...
    fn run(
        &mut self,
        (mut balls, players, transforms): Self::SystemData
    ) {
        for (ball, transform) in (&mut balls, &transforms).join() {
            // ...

            // Bounce at the players.
            for (player, player_transform) in
                (&players, &transforms).join() {
                let player_x = player_transform
                    .translation().x - (player.width * 0.5);
                let player_y = player_transform
                    .translation().y - (player.height * 0.5);
                if point_in_rect(
                    ball_x,
                    ball_y,
                    player_x - ball.radius,
                    player_y - ball.radius,
                    player_x + player.width + ball.radius,
                    player_y + player.height + ball.radius,
                ) {
                    if ball.velocity[1] < 0.0 {
                        // Only bounce when ball is falling
                        ball.velocity[1] = -ball.velocity[1];

                        let mut rng = rand::thread_rng();
                        match player.side {
```

```
                            Side::Left => {
                                ball.velocity[0] =
                                    ball.velocity[0].abs() *
                                    rng.gen_range(0.6, 1.4)
                            }
                            Side::Right => {
                                ball.velocity[0] =
                                    -ball.velocity[0].abs() *
                                    rng.gen_range(0.6, 1.4)
                            }
                        }
                    }
                }
            }
        }
    }
}
```

Keeping Score

The game is now fully playable, but you have to keep the score by paper and pen. To make the game keep the score for you, you simply need to create another system, as you might have guessed. First, you need to set up the skeleton code for the WinnerSystem, as shown in in Listing 4-26.

Listing 4-26. The Winner System

```
// src/systems/winner.rs
use amethyst::{
    core::transform::Transform,
    core::SystemDesc,
```

```
    derive::SystemDesc,
    ecs::prelude::{Join, System, SystemData, World, WriteStorage},
};

use crate::catvolleyball::{Ball, ARENA_HEIGHT, ARENA_WIDTH};

#[derive(SystemDesc)]
pub struct WinnerSystem;

impl<'s> System<'s> for WinnerSystem {
    // ...
}

// src/systems/mod.rs
// ...
mod winner;
pub use self::winner::WinnerSystem;

// src/main.rs
// ...
let game_data = GameDataBuilder::default()
    // ...
    .with(systems::WinnerSystem, "winner_system", &["ball_system"])
    // ...
```

Inside the run() function of the WinnerSystem, you are going to use the following algorithm to determine the winner:

1. If the ball touches the bottom boundary (i.e., the ball's center is less than one radius above the ground), it's a goal.

2. Check the ball's x coordinate to see if it's on the left side or the right side of the arena. If it's on the right side, the left player wins, and vice versa.

3. Reposition the ball in the center of the arena. Reset
    the ball's Y-axis velocity to zero. Reverse the ball's
    X-axis velocity to make the ball shoot toward the
    winner's side; this simulates the change of the right
    of serve.

This code can be easily implemented in Listing 4-27.

Listing 4-27. The Winner System Algorithm

```rust
impl<'s> System<'s> for WinnerSystem {
    type SystemData = (WriteStorage<'s, Ball>,
        WriteStorage<'s, Transform>);

    fn run(&mut self, (mut balls, mut locals): Self::SystemData) {
        for (ball, transform) in (&mut balls, &mut locals).join() {
            let ball_x = transform.translation().x;
            let ball_y = transform.translation().y;

            if ball_y <= ball.radius {
                // touched the ground
                if ball_x <= (ARENA_WIDTH / 2.0) {
                    println!("Right player scored");

                } else {
                    println!("Left player scored");
                }

                // reset the ball to the middle
                transform.set_translation_x(ARENA_WIDTH / 2.0);
                transform.set_translation_y(ARENA_HEIGHT / 2.0);
                // reverse the direction
                ball.velocity[0] = -ball.velocity[0];
                ball.velocity[1] = 0.0; // reset to free drop
```

```
            }
        }
    }
}
```

In Listing 4-27, you only print who scored, but you can't expect the
gamer to look at the log file of the game. It's better to show the score
directly on the screen using the UI system. To use the UI system, you are
going to add the UiBundle to the rendering pipeline (see Listing 4-28).

Listing 4-28. Loading the UI Bundle

```
// src/main.rs
// ...
use amethyst::ui::{RenderUi, UiBundle}
// ...

fn main() -> amethyst::Result<()> {
    // ...

    let game_data = GameDataBuilder::default()
        // ...
        .with_bundle(UiBundle::<StringBindings>::new())?
        .with_bundle(
            RenderingBundle::<DefaultBackend>::new()
                // ... other plugins
                .with_plugin(RenderUi::default()),
        )?;
    // ...
}
```

You add the UiBundle to the GameDataBuilder. You also add the RenderUi
plugin to the RenderingBundler. First, you need to create a system data
struct to hold the score, so you can create one in src/cat_volleyball.rs:

```
#[derive(Default)]
pub struct ScoreBoard {
    pub score_left: i32,
    pub score_right: i32,
}
```

Then in the WinnerSystem, you can store the data in this struct instead of printing it to the log (see Listing 4-29). You then increment the score by one every time they score and cap the number to 999, so the text won't overflow the screen.

Listing 4-29. Keeping the Score in ScoreBoard

```
// ...
use amethyst::ecs::prelude::{Join, System, SystemData,
    World, Write, WriteStorage},
use crate::catvolleyball::{ScoreBoard}

#[derive(SystemDesc)]
pub struct WinnerSystem;

impl<'s> System<'s> for WinnerSystem {
    type SystemData = (
        WriteStorage<'s, Ball>,
        WriteStorage<'s, Transform>,
        Write<'s, ScoreBoard>,
    );

    fn run(
        &mut self,
        (mut balls, mut locals, mut scores): Self::SystemData,
    ) {
        for (ball, transform) in (&mut balls, &mut locals).join() {
            // ...
```

```
    if ball_y <= ball.radius {
        // touched the ground
        if ball_x <= (ARENA_WIDTH / 2.0) {
            scores.score_right =
                (scores.score_right + 1).min(999);
        } else {
            scores.score_left =
                (scores.score_left + 1).min(999);
        }

        // reset the ball to the middle ...
        }
    }
  }
}
```

Now that you have the score ready, you can show it on the screen with two UiText entities (see Listing 4-30). In src/catvolleyball.rs, you first create a ScoreText struct that holds the two UiText entities for the left and right player's score. Then you add an initialize_scoreboard() function that does the actual initialization, which you'll invoke in the on_start() function of the main game state.

Listing 4-30. Initializing the UiText Entities

```
use amethyst::ecs::prelude::{Entity};
use amethyst::ui::{Anchor, TtfFormat, UiText, UiTransform};

pub struct ScoreText {
    pub p1_score: Entity,
    pub p2_score: Entity,
}
```

```
fn initialize_scoreboard(world: &mut World) {
    let font = world.read_resource::<Loader>().load(
        "font/square.ttf",
        TtfFormat,
        (),
        &world.read_resource(),
    );

    let p1_transform = UiTransform::new(
        "P1".to_string(),   // ID
        Anchor::TopMiddle,  // anchor
        Anchor::Middle,     // pivot
        -50.,               // x
        -50.,               // y
        1.,                 // z
        200.,               // width
        50.,                // height
    );
    let p2_transform = UiTransform::new(
        "P2".to_string(),
        Anchor::TopMiddle,
        Anchor::Middle,
        50.,
        -50.,
        1.,
        200.,
        50.,
    );

    let p1_score = world
        .create_entity()
        .with(p1_transform)
```

```
        .with(UiText::new(
            font.clone(),
            "0".to_string(),  // initial text: 0 points
            [1., 1., 1., 1.], // color (RGBA): white
            50.,              // font size
        ))
        .build();

    let p2_score = world
        .create_entity()
        .with(p2_transform)
        .with(UiText::new(
            font.clone(),
            "0".to_string(),
            [1., 1., 1., 1.],
            50.,
        ))
        .build();

    world.insert(ScoreText { p1_score, p2_score });
}

pub struct CatVolleyball;

impl SimpleState for CatVolleyball {
    fn on_start(&mut self, data: StateData<'_, GameData<'_, '_>>) {
        // ...
        initialize_scoreboard(world);
    }
}
```

The UiText entity needs a font to display the text, so you put a font called square.ttf in assets/font/, then load it with world.read_ resource::<Loader>().load(). Then you have to set up two transforms, which will place the text 50 pixels below the top-middle point of the window, one 50 pixels left of the center and the other 50 pixels right of the center. Then you create two UiText entities with the initial text "0" and make them white. These two Entities are then wrapped in a ScoreText struct and added to the world.

Finally, you have to update the UiText every time the WinnerSystem detects a win. You can easily add the ScoreText to the SystemData and update the UiText right after you update the score in ScoreBoard (see Listing 4-31). The UiText will look like Figure 4-12.

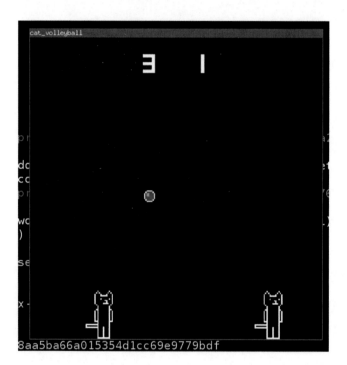

Figure 4-12. *Showing the score*

Listing 4-31. Updating the Score on the UI in the WinnerSystem

```
// ...
new ecs::prelude::{Join, ReadExpect, System, SystemData, World,
    Write, WriteStorage},
```

```rust
impl<'s> System<'s> for WinnerSystem {
    type SystemData = (
        WriteStorage<'s, Ball>,
        WriteStorage<'s, Transform>,
        WriteStorage<'s, UiText>,
        Write<'s, ScoreBoard>,
        ReadExpect<'s, ScoreText>,
    );

    fn run(
        &mut self,
        (mut balls, mut locals, mut ui_text,
         mut scores, score_text): Self::SystemData,
    ) {
        for (ball, transform) in (&mut balls, &mut locals).join() {
            // ...
                if ball_y <= ball.radius {
                    if ball_x <= (ARENA_WIDTH / 2.0) {
                        scores.score_right =
                            (scores.score_right + 1).min(999);

                        // Update the UI's text content
                        if let Some(text) = ui_text
                            .get_mut(score_text.p2_score) {
                            text.text = scores.score_right
                                .to_string();
                        }
                    } else {
                        scores.score_left =
                            (scores.score_left + 1).min(999);
```

```
            if let Some(text) = ui_text
                .get_mut(score_text.p1_score) {
                text.text = scores.score_left
                    .to_string();
            }
        }
        // ...
    }
}
}
```

Let There Be Music

Now you have a complete game, but it doesn't feel complete without
sound effects and background music. To be able to play music in the game,
you need to add the AudioBundle to the GameData in src/main.rs (see
Listing 4-32).

Listing 4-32. Loading the AudioBundle

```
use amethyst::audio::{AudioBundle};

fn main() -> amethyst::Result<()> {
    // ...
    let game_data = GameDataBuilder::default()
        // ...
        .with_bundle(AudioBundle::default())?
        // ...
}
```

Then you need to load the audio files into data structures that are friendly to the Amethyst audio systems. You could add them to the src/catvolleyball.rs file, but the file is already quite big. So instead, you'll create a new Rust module to hold all the audio-related code and reference it in src/catvolleyball.rs and src/main.rs. Let's create the src/audio.rs file and create some function that will load the background music (see Listing 4-33).

Listing 4-33. Audio Module for Loading the Background Music

```
// src/catvolleyball.rs
// ...
use crate::audio::initialize_audio;

pub const AUDIO_MUSIC: &'static [&'static str] = &[
    "./audio/Computer_Music_All-Stars_-_Wheres_My_Jetpack.ogg",
    "./audio/Computer_Music_All-Stars_-_Albatross_v2.ogg",
];
pub const AUDIO_BOUNCE: &'static str = "./audio/bounce.ogg";
pub const AUDIO_SCORE: &'static str = "./audio/score.ogg";

// ...

pub struct CatVolleyball;

impl SimpleState for CatVolleyball {
    fn on_start(&mut self, data: StateData<'_, GameData<'_, '_>>) {
        // ...
        initialize_audio(world);
    }
}
```

143

```rust
// src/audio.rs
use amethyst::{
    assets::{AssetStorage, Loader},
    audio::{output::Output, AudioSink, OggFormat, Source,
        SourceHandle},
    ecs::prelude::{World, WorldExt},
};

use std::iter::Cycle;
use std::vec::IntoIter;

pub struct Music { // background music tracks
    pub music: Cycle<IntoIter<SourceHandle>>,
}

pub struct Sounds { // sound effects
    pub score_sfx: SourceHandle,
    pub bounce_sfx: SourceHandle,
}

/// Loads an ogg audio track.
fn load_audio_track(loader: &Loader, world: &World, file: &str)
    -> SourceHandle {
    loader.load(file, OggFormat, (), &world.read_resource())
}

pub fn initialize_audio(world: &mut World) {
    use crate::catvolleyball::{AUDIO_BOUNCE, AUDIO_MUSIC,
        AUDIO_SCORE};

    let (sound_effects, music) = {
        let mut sink = world.write_resource::<AudioSink>();
        // Music is a bit loud, reduce the volume.
        sink.set_volume(0.25);

        let loader = world.read_resource::<Loader>();
```

```
        let music = AUDIO_MUSIC
            .iter()
            .map(|file| load_audio_track(&loader, &world, file))
            .collect::<Vec<_>>()
            .into_iter()
            .cycle();
        let music = Music { music };

        let sound = Sounds {
            bounce_sfx: load_audio_track(&loader, &world,
                AUDIO_BOUNCE),
            score_sfx: load_audio_track(&loader, &world,
                AUDIO_SCORE),
        };

        (sound, music)
    };

    /* Add sound effects to the world. We have to do this in
       another scope because world won't let us insert
       new resources as long as 'Loader' is borrowed. */
    world.insert(sound_effects);
    world.insert(music);
}
```

You create a src/audio.rs file and reference it in src/catvolleyball.
rs using use. Then you define the .ogg music files' paths in the constants
AUDIO_MUSIC, AUDIO_BOUNCE, and AUDIO_SCORE. In src/audio.rs,
you first define two structs to hold the loaded audio file: Music and
Sounds. The Sounds struct is relatively simple; it has a score_sfx field,
which is the sound effect for scoring a win, and bounce_sfx for the ball
bouncing sound. Music is an iterator of soundtracks, but you wrap it in an
std::iter::Cycle so the soundtracks will keep looping endlessly.

You then create a helper function called `load_audio_track()` that will help you load the audio .ogg audio file in the `SourceHandle`. As usual, you create an `initialize_audio()` function and call it in the game state's `on_start()` function. The `initialize_audio()` function first creates an `AudioSink`. Think of it as a programmatical way to control a music player. It has function like `.play()`, `.pause()`, `.stop()`, and `.set_volume()`, which are typical things you'll expect from a music player interface. Then you use the `load_audio_track()` helper function to load the files specified in `AUDIO_MUSIC`, `AUDIO_BOUNCE`, and `AUDIO_SCORE` into their corresponding data structures. Finally, you add them to the `world` as resources.

Now you have an `AudioSink` that can load play music, and you have all the .ogg tracks loaded, but how do you play the music in a loop? This is when the `DjSystem` comes in handy. The `DjSystem` will call a user-defined closure whenever the `AudioSink` is not playing anymore. This is why you put the soundtracks in a `Cycle` iterator. When the `DjSystem` detects the last track stops, it can call the `.next()` function on the iterator to get the next track and play it. Because the `Cycle` iterator will loop forever, you'll never run out of music. Because the `DjSystem` needs to initialize an audio output device and put the device into the `World`, you can just add the `DjSystem` with `GameDataBuilder.with()`. You need to utilize the `SystemDesc` trait and use `DjSystemDesc` instead. The code for loading the `DjSystemDesc` will look like Listing 4-34.

Listing 4-34. Loading the DjSystemDesc

```
// src/main.rs
use amethyst::audio::{AudioBundle, DySystemDesc};

mod audio;
use crate::audio::Music;
```

```
fn main() -> amethyst::Result<()> {
    // ...
    let game_data = GameDataBuilder::default()
        // ...
        .with_bundle(AudioBundle::default())?
        .with(
            DjSystemDesc::new(
                |music: &mut Music| music.music.next()
            ),
            "dj_system",
            &[],
        )
        // ...
}
```

Next, you can add some sound effects when the ball collides to make it more realistic. Since you already loaded the sound effect audio files in src/audio.rs, you need to expose some functions to the WinnerSystem so it can play the sounds at the right time. In the src/audio.rs file, you add the following two functions (see Listing 4-35).

Listing 4-35. Functions to Play the Sound Effects

```
// src/audio.rs
/// Plays the bounce sound when a ball hits a side or a paddle.
pub fn play_bounce(
    sounds: &Sounds,
    storage: &AssetStorage<Source>,
    output: Option<&Output>
) {
```

```
    if let Some(ref output) = output.as_ref() {
        if let Some(sound) = storage.get(&sounds.bounce_sfx) {
            output.play_once(sound, 1.0);
        }
    }
}

/// Plays the score sound when a player scores
pub fn play_score(
    sounds: &Sounds,
    storage: &AssetStorage<Source>,
    output: Option<&Output>
) {
    if let Some(ref output) = output.as_ref() {
        if let Some(sound) = storage.get(&sounds.score_sfx) {
            output.play_once(sound, 1.0);
        }
    }
}
```

Then in the BounceSystem, you need to play this sound when the ball bounces (see Listing 4-36).

Listing 4-36. Playing the Bounce Sound Effect in the BounceSystem

```
use amethyst::{
    assets::AssetStorage,
    audio::{output::Output, Source},
    core::transform::Transform,
    core::SystemDesc,
    derive::SystemDesc,
    ecs::prelude::{Join, Read, ReadExpect, ReadStorage, System,
        SystemData, World, WriteStorage},
};
```

```rust
use std::ops::Deref;

use crate::audio::{play_bounce, Sounds};

#[derive(SystemDesc)]
pub struct BounceSystem;

impl<'s> System<'s> for BounceSystem {
    type SystemData = (
        WriteStorage<'s, Ball>,
        ReadStorage<'s, Player>,
        ReadStorage<'s, Transform>,
        Read<'s, AssetStorage<Source>>, // for sound
        ReadExpect<'s, Sounds>,         // for sound
        Option<Read<'s, Output>>,       // for sound
    );

    fn run(
        &mut self,
        (mut balls, players, transforms, storage, sounds,
         audio_output): Self::SystemData) {
        for (ball, transform) in (&mut balls, &transforms).join() {
            // ...

            // Bounce at the four sides of the arena.
            if ball_y <= ball.radius && ball.velocity[1] < 0.0 {
                ball.velocity[1] = -ball.velocity[1];
                // Don't play the sound since we are going to
                // play the score sound
            } else if ball_y >= (ARENA_HEIGHT - ball.radius)
                && ball.velocity[1] > 0.0 {
                ball.velocity[1] = -ball.velocity[1];
```

```
        play_bounce(
            &*sounds,
            &storage,
            audio_output.as_ref().map(|o| o.deref())
        );
    } else if ball_x <= ball.radius && ball.velocity[0] < 0.0 {
        ball.velocity[0] = -ball.velocity[0];
        play_bounce(
            &*sounds,
            &storage,
            audio_output.as_ref().map(|o| o.deref())
        );
    } else if ball_x >= (ARENA_WIDTH - ball.radius)
        && ball.velocity[0] > 0.0 {
        ball.velocity[0] = -ball.velocity[0];
        play_bounce(
            &*sounds,
            &storage,
            audio_output.as_ref().map(|o| o.deref())
        );
    }
}

// Bounce at the players.
for (player, player_transform) in
    (&players, &transforms).join() {
    // ...
    if point_in_rect(
        // ...
    ) {
        if ball.velocity[1] < 0.0 {
            // Only bounce when ball is falling
            ball.velocity[1] = -ball.velocity[1];
```

```
            // ... invert the ball velocity
            play_bounce(
                &*sounds,
                &storage,
                audio_output.as_ref().map(|o|o.deref())
            );
        }
      }
    }
  }
}
```

Notice that in the BounceSystem, you add three more SystemData—
AssetStorage<Source>, Sounds, and Output—so you can use the sound in
the system. Then you call the play_bounce() function whenever the ball
bounces. You should deliberately skip the bounce sound when the ball
hits the ground because you are going to play the score sound effect in the
WinnerSystem instead.

Playing the score sound is almost the same as playing the bounce
sound. In src/systems/winner.rs, you simply add the SystemData
required for the sound effect and call the play_score() function when the
ball hits the ground (see Listing 4-37).

Listing 4-37. Playing the Score Sound Effect in the WinnerSystem

```
use amethyst::{
    // ...
    ecs::prelude::{Join, Read, ReadExpect, System, SystemData,
        World, Write, WriteStorage},
};
```

```rust
use crate::audio::{play_score, Sounds};
use std::ops::Deref;

#[derive(SystemDesc)]
pub struct WinnerSystem;

impl<'s> System<'s> for WinnerSystem {
    type SystemData = (
        WriteStorage<'s, Ball>,
        WriteStorage<'s, Transform>,
        WriteStorage<'s, UiText>,
        Write<'s, ScoreBoard>,
        ReadExpect<'s, ScoreText>,
        Read<'s, AssetStorage<Source>>, // for sound
        ReadExpect<'s, Sounds>,         // for sound
        Option<Read<'s, Output>>,       // for sound
    );

    fn run(
        &mut self,
        (mut balls, mut locals, mut ui_text,
         mut scores, score_text, storage, sounds,
         audio_output): Self::SystemData,
    ) {
        for (ball, transform) in (&mut balls, &mut locals).join() {
            // ...

            if ball_y <= ball.radius { // touched the ground

                // ... decide who wins
                // ... reset the ball to the middle
```

```
play_score(
    &*sounds,
    &storage,
    audio_output.as_ref().map(|o| o.deref())
);
        }
    }
  }
}
```

Finally, you have a working game! You learned how to create a render pipeline to render players and the ball on the screen using the spritesheet. Then you added keyboard controls so you could control the players. You added a few systems to handle simple physics like gravity and bouncing. You learned how to keep the score using the WinnerSystem and display the score using some UiTexts. Lastly, you added background music and sound effects to the game to spice it up.

Other Alternatives

In terms of a full-fledged game engine, the most popular ones on crates. io are probably Amethyst, Piston, and ggez. However, the development of Piston is less active than Amethyst at the moment. Ggez took a different path and focused only on 2D games. However, these game engines are relatively young compared to commercial ones like Unity and Unreal. They are also relatively immature compared to the commonly used libraries like SDL2 and OpenGL. Therefore, you can also choose to use Rust bindings for existing libraries. As Michael Fairley, the author of the Rust game "A Snake's Tale," demonstrated in his blog post[7], you can build a game using

---

[7]https://michaelfairley.com/blog/i-made-a-game-in-rust/

Rust bindings to libraries like SDL2 and OpenGL. You can also choose your crate for doing math, image, and font rendering. You'll need more experience to put these things together. However, if you're an experienced game developer who is familiar with these libraries in other languages (e.g., C/C++), this might be an easy way to get up to speed.

Note   You'll find that the Rust community loves to track the progress of a certain area using their "Are We X Yet" sites. This is a tradition from the Mozilla community, which many Rustaceans are also involved in. Whenever there is a big project or a certain goal that people want to track, someone will build an "Are We X Yet" site to track it. You can find a list of all the "Are We X Yet" sites at `https://wiki.mozilla.org/Areweyet`.

The game ecosystem in Rust is still in its early stages. As in many other fields of Rust, there is an "Are We X Yet" page that tracks the progress of the game development ecosystem. See `http://arewegameyet.com/`. On this website, you'll find many useful crates that can fulfill your game development needs. You'll also find a list of games built with Rust. If you are unsure about which game engine to choose, it's a good idea to look at the existing games and figure out which libraries they used.

CHAPTER 5

Physical Computing in Rust

Up until now, all the programs you have written exist only in the virtual world. However, a big part of the physical world is controlled by software. Traffic lights, self-driving cars, airplanes, and even rockets and satellites are just a few examples. Much of this software has to be compiled and executed in a drastically different environment than the usual Linux, Windows, or MacOS desktop or laptop computers. They usually have to run on relatively weaker CPUs with less available memories. They might sometimes need to run without an operating system, or on specialized operating systems designed specifically for embedded systems.

Traditionally, these applications are written in C or C++ for maximum performance and low-level control of memory. Many of the embedded platforms are so limited that garbage collection is not feasible. But this is where Rust shines. Rust can provide performance and low-level control as C or C++ but it guarantees higher safety. A Rust program can be compiled to run on many different CPUs, like Intel, ARM, and MIPS. It also supports various mainstream operating systems and even no operating systems.

© Shing Lyu 2020
S. Lyu, *Practical Rust Projects*, https://doi.org/10.1007/978-1-4842-5599-5_5

What Are You Building?

This chapter focuses on using Rust on a Raspberry Pi. Raspberry Pi is an inexpensive computer with a credit card size footprint, created to make computer education more accessible. It has a few key important features that demonstrate the points in this chapter:

- It has an ARM CPU. You can learn how to compile and cross-compile code for an ARM platform.

- It has GPIO pins. You can use them to control physical circuits like LEDs and buttons.

- It's powerful enough to run a full Debian-based operating system (Raspbian), so you can learn about physical computing and cross-compilation without going too deep into bare-metal programming. But if you are feeling adventurous, you can try writing your own mini operating system on it with Rust.

To begin with, you'll install a full operating system on the Raspberry Pi. Then you'll install the complete Rust toolchain on it. You'll build two circuits, one for output and one for input, and use Rust to interact with them:

- *Output:* The first circuit will allow you to generate output to the physical world with light. You'll create a simple LED circuit connected to a GPIO output pin. You can write a Rust program to turn the LED on and off and blink it regularly.

- *Input:* You can take input from the physical world as well. You'll add a pushbutton to the circuit. The Rust program can detect button clicks and then toggle the LED on and off.

These two examples will help you gain an understanding of how Rust code interacts with the physical world. However, you will compile them on the Raspberry Pi itself. In many embedded applications, the target platform (i.e., the Raspberry Pi or similar board) is not powerful enough to compile the code. Therefore, you'll move the compilation to another computer, which is more powerful but has a different CPU and OS than the target platform. This way of compiling is called *cross-compilation.* You'll set up a cross-compilation toolchain and cross-compile the previous example on it. Finally, to give you a sneak-peek into how the GPIO pin works, you'll use lower-level APIs to control it. You'll be able to get a sense of how the high-level GPIO libraries work.

Physical Computing on Raspberry Pi
Getting to Know Your Raspberry Pi

You'll be using a Raspberry Pi 3 B+ board for this chapter, as shown in Figure 5-1.

Figure 5-1. *Raspberry Pi 3 B+*

A Raspberry Pi board is like a mini-computer. It has all the necessary components of a computer: CPU, memory, WiFi, Bluetooth, HDMI output, USB, etc.

One significant difference between Raspberry Pi and a typical desktop or laptop computer is that it uses an ARM CPU. Most of the mainstream desktop or laptop computers nowadays use the Intel x86/x86_64 architecture CPUs. However, ARM CPUs are more common in mobile, embedded, and IoT devices due to lower power consumption. Since Rust is a language that compiles to machine code, the CPU architecture dictates how the final output is.

Raspberry Pi features many peripherals. It has an SD card reader so you can load your program and an operating system onto an SD card. It has a micro-USB power input so it can run on a phone charger or even a portable power bank. For video output, you can use its HDMI output to connect to an HDMI monitor. To control the device, you can use a USB mouse and keyboard. Finally, you can see two rows of metal pins (on the top-left edge of Figure 5-1). These are GPIO (General-Purpose Input/ Output) pins, which you'll use in the later chapters to interact with external circuits like LEDs and buttons.

Install Raspbian Through NOOBS

In the first example, you are going to see how to run a Rust program on an operating system. There are many operating systems available for Raspberry Pi. What you need to do is to install an operating system image onto the SD card and let the Raspberry Pi boot from the image. The official Raspberry Pi operating system is called Raspbian. Raspbian is a Debian-based operating system that has a friendly desktop environment and many useful software packages like the Firefox browser, text editor, calculator, and also programming environments for education, like Scratch, Python, Java, etc.

The easiest way to install Raspbian is to use an installer called *NOOBS* (New Out Of the Box Software). It provides a step-by-step wizard to guide you through the installation process. Here are the steps:

1. Head to the NOOBS download page `https://www.raspberrypi.org/downloads/noobs/` (see Figure 5-2) and download the ZIP file for *Offline and Network Install.*

2. Prepare an SD card (at least 8GB), formatted to the FAT format.

3. Unzip the NOOBS ZIP file and copy all the files to the SD card.

4. Plug the SD card in to the Raspberry Pi.

5. Connect your Raspberry Pi with a keyboard, mouse, and an HDMI monitor.

6. Connect your Raspberry Pi with a micro-USB power source (usually a phone/tablet charger). This will turn the Raspberry Pi on.

7. Once the NOOB installer has booted, you can select the Raspbian option from the menu. NOOBS will start the installation process.

8. Once it's installed, you can reboot the Raspberry Pi, and the Raspbian OS is ready.

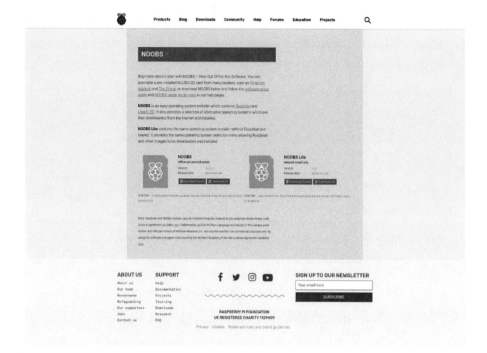

Figure 5-2. *The NOOBS download page*

Note   If you don't want to install the operating system yourself, you can also buy a pre-installed SD card from many electronics stores or educational stores online.

Install the Rust Toolchain

As you did for the Linux desktop, you can install the Rust compiler and cargo on the Raspbian with rustup. Run the following command, copied from the Rust official installation page at https://www.rust-lang.org/tools/install:

```
curl https://sh.rustup.rs -sSf | sh
```

This will install the whole Rust toolchain on your Raspberry Pi. One big difference you might notice is that `rustup` detects the ARM CPU and suggests a different target architecture `armv7-unknown-linux-gnueabihf` (see Figure 5-3). You want `rustc` to compile the Rust code into the ARM assembly so that the binary can run on the Raspberry Pi. Therefore, you should take `rustup`'s suggestion and install the toolchain for ARM. Once it's installed, don't forget to add the `cargo` folder to the PATH environment variable, so that the `cargo` command will work.

```
Current installation options:

    default host triple: armv7-unknown-linux-gnueabihf
      default toolchain: stable
                profile: default
   modify PATH variable: yes

1) Proceed with installation (default)
2) Customize installation
3) Cancel installation
>
```

Figure 5-3. *Rustup suggests installing the ARM target*

Controlling the GPIO Pins

Once you set the stage for Raspberry Pi, you are going to look at two rows of metal pins that occupy one side of the circuit board. These pins are called GPIO (general-purpose input/output) pins. These GPIO pins are used to communicate with the outside world. When a pin acts as an output, you can control it with software to let it output either 3.3 volts (written as 3V3) or 0 volts. When a pin works as an input, it can detect whether the pin voltage is high (3V3) or low (0V).

Not all pins are used as input/output pins. Some pins have special purposes like consistently providing 5V power, or working as the ground (constant 0V). Figure 5-4 shows the layout of the pins. You can also find an interactive pin layout at `https://pinout.xyz/`.

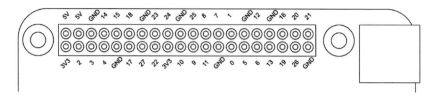

Figure 5-4. *Raspberry Pi 3 B+ GPIO layout (BCM numbering)*

There are a few different kinds of pins:

- 5V: 5V power supply

- 3V3: 3.3V power supply

- GND: ground

- Number: With a GPIO pin, the number is the BCM number. When you refer to pin by its number in the example code, you are referring to this number[1]

Some pins can also be configured to communicate using particular protocols, like PWM (Pulse-Width Modulation), SPI (Serial Peripheral Interface), I²C (Inter-Integrated Circuit) or Serial, which you'll not use in this book.

On a very high level, these GPIO pins are controlled by hardware registers. Registers are components in the chip that act like computer memory. You can read or write bits to them. To set the mode (input, output, or special protocol) of a pin, you can write a specific bit pattern to some register. These registers are exposed as memory addresses (`/dev/gpiomem`), so you can change their value as if you were writing to a particular memory location. But direct manipulation of memory is too low level for most use

---

[1]You might find the number confusing because they seem random. BCM refers to the "Broadcom SOC channel," which is the internal numbering of pins in the Broadcom brand CPU used by the Raspberry Pi. Some Raspberry Pi GPIO libraries also support the "board" numbering, which is the sequential numbering, left to right, bottom to top, from 1 to 40.

cases, so there are a few abstractions on top of that. On the Raspbian OS, these registers are exposed as device files (`/sys/class/gpio/*`)[2]. You can read from these virtual files to get the register's value. If you write to these files like regular files, the register will be set accordingly.

But manipulating these virtual files is still very tedious. To further conceal the complexity, you can use the `rust_gpiozero` crate. The `rust_gpiozero` crate is inspired by the Python `gpiozero` library, which exposes easy-to-use components like `LED` or `Button` so you can control these GPIO-connected hardware components with ease. The `rust_gpiozero` crate is built on top of the `rppal` (Raspberry Pi Peripheral Access Library) crate, which allows low-level access to various peripherals like the GPIO pins.

To start using `rust_gpiozero`, simply go to your Raspberry Pi desktop, open the terminal, and create a new project by typing `cargo new physical-computing`. Then you add the following to the generated `Cargo.toml` file:

```
[dependencies]
rust_gpiozero = "0.2.0"
```

Now the software environment is ready. You can start connecting the hardware circuits and start coding.

Building a LED Circuit

First, you need to light up an LED (light-emitting diode) (see Figure 5-5). An LED is a small electronic component that will emit light when electrical current flows through it. The "D" in LED stands for *diode*, which means it only allows the electrical current to flow in one direction. The positive leg is called the *anode*, which is usually the longer leg of the two. The negative leg is called the *cathode*. You can give a high voltage to the anode, say 3.3V, and ground the cathode. This will create a current flowing from the anode to the cathode, and the LED will light up.

---

[2]They are provided by `Sysfs`, a Linux virtual filesystem.

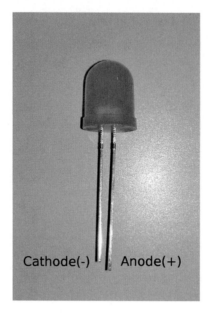

Cathode(-)   Anode(+)

Figure 5-5. *A yellow LED*

Tip   As mentioned, the LED works in only one direction. If your LED is not lighting up, don't panic. Try swapping the direction of the LED, and it will probably work.

Although Raspberry Pi doesn't provide a very high voltage and current, it's still possible that too much current will pass through the LED and break it. To protect against such a scenario, you can add a resistor (see Figure 5-6) into the circuit. A resistor creates resistance to the current, effectively limiting the current that goes through the LED.

It's pretty hard to work with free-floating LEDs and resistors by just connecting them with wires. You'll probably need to solder them together, but then it's hard to break them apart and rearrange. To make it easier to work with experimental circuits, you can use a breadboard (see Figure 5-6). A breadboard is a plastic board with tiny holes that LEDs, wires, and other electronic parts can plug into. Inside the holes are rows of metal pieces that act as temporary wires. A breadboard is perfect for prototyping because you can easily plug electronic parts and form a circuit. You can easily unplug them if you make any mistakes. You'll also be using jumper wires to connect the circuits. A jumper wire is a pre-cut wire with rigid plastic and metal heads on each end. The head makes it easy to plug the wire into the breadboard and makes them more durable than raw, unprotected wires.

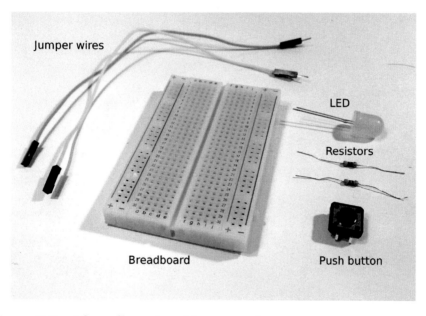

Figure 5-6. *A breadboard and jumper wires*

Now you'll connect a circuit like the diagram in Figure 5-7. A photo is shown in Figure 5-8. In this circuit, the electric current goes from GPIO pin 2 to the anode leg of the LED (connected through the breadboard) and comes out of the cathode leg. The current then goes through the current-limiting resistor, and to the ground rail (the column on the breadboard that is marked blue with a - logo), and then finally goes to the ground GPIO pin. You can turn the LED on and off by setting the GPIO pin 2 to high (3V3) or low (0V) with Rust.

Controlling the GPIO Output from Rust

You already created a Rust project and added the rust_gpiozero crates to the dependencies. The rust_gpiozero page makes it really simple to control the GPIO pins. Open src/main.rs and write the code shown in Listing 5-1.

Listing 5-1. Turning the LED On

```rust
extern crate rust_gpiozero;
use rust_gpiozero::*;

fn main() {
    let mut led = LED::new(2);

    led.on();
}
```

You can compile and run this code on the Raspberry Pi by running cargo run. The compilation might take longer because the Raspberry Pi ARM CPU might not be as powerful as your desktop or laptop computer's CPU. If your circuit is connected correctly, you should see the LED light up.

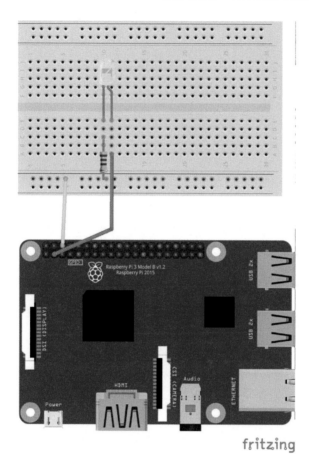

Figure 5-7. *The LED circuit diagram (image created with Fritzing)*

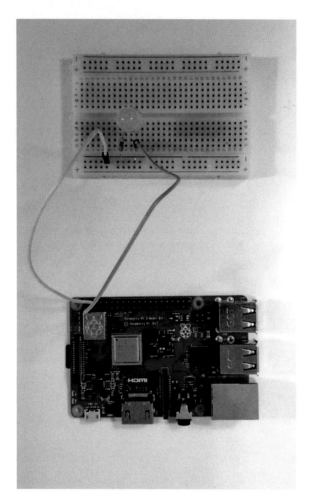

Figure 5-8. *The LED circuit*

In Listing 5-1, you initiate an LED. The integer parameter is the GPIO pin number that this LED should control. During initiation, `rust_gpiozero` will set the GPIO pin in the output mode for you automatically. Then when you call `led.on()`, it will set the correct bit in the register and make the GPIO pin go high (3.3V), which turns the LED on. As you might have guessed, the way to turn off this LED is as simple as changing the code to `led.off()` and running `cargo run` again.

If you want to flash the LED, you can use a loop and add a one second pause between led.on() and led.off(). The pause can be easily achieved by sleep(Duration::from_secs(1)), provided by the standard library. The complete code for it is shown in Listing 5-2.

Listing 5-2. A Naive Implementation of Blinking the LED

```rust
extern crate rust_gpiozero;
use rust_gpiozero::*;
use std::thread::sleep;
use std::time::Duration;

fn main() {
    let led = LED::new(2);

    loop{
        println!("on");
        led.on();

        sleep(Duration::from_secs(1));

        println!("off");
        led.off();

        sleep(Duration::from_secs(1));
    }
}
```

To make it even simpler, rust_gpiozero already implemented flashing for you. You can use the LED::blink() function, as shown in Listing 5-3.

Listing 5-3. Blink Using rust_gpiozero LED::blink()

```rust
extern crate rust_gpiozero;
use rust_gpiozero::*;
```

```rust
fn main() {
    let mut led = LED::new(2);

    led.blink(1.0, 1.0);

    led.wait(); // Prevents the program from exiting
}
```

The LED::blink() function takes two parameters: on_time and off_time. The on_time parameter is how many seconds the LED should stay on; the off_time parameter is how many seconds to pause in between. You also have to call the LED::wait() function to prevent the program from exiting right after the LED::blink() call.

Reading Button Clicks

Now you have learned how to output a light signal from the software world to the physical world. You can now see how to accept physical inputs. You can configure the GPIO pin to use the input mode and receive inputs from a physical button.

The GPIO input pin can be configured to detect the voltage and trigger the code when the voltage reaches the desired level. However, the GPIO input pin by itself will not stay at either 0V or 3V3. It will be in a *floating* state where its voltage is between 0V and 3V3, which makes it prone to false-trigger. Fortunately, the Raspberry Pi has an internal resistor that can be configured to keep the GPIO pin at 0V or 3V3. These resistors are tagged as the "pull-down resistor" and "pull-up resistor" in Figures 5-9 and 5-10. When you enable the pull-down resistor, it will connect the pin to the ground, thus pulling the voltage down to 0V. When you enable the pull-up resistor, it will connect the pin to an internal 3V3 voltage source and pull the voltage up to 3V3.

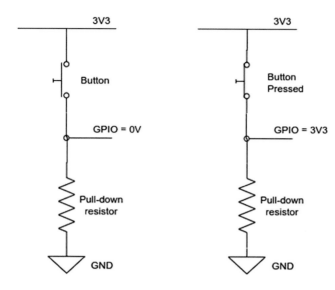

Figure 5-9. *Input pin with an internal pull-down resistor*

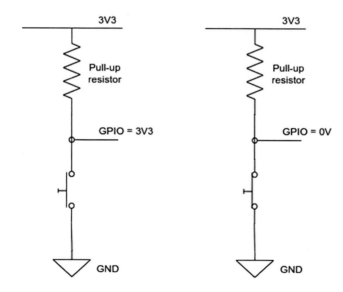

Figure 5-10. *Input pin with an internal pull-up resistor*

You can imagine a button as two pieces of separated metal, so no current will flow through it when it's not pressed. When you press the button, the two pieces of metal touch and short-circuit, allowing the current to flow through. Since the GPIO input pin can detect a voltage change, you can use the GPIO pins to detect a button press in two ways:

- Configure the GPIO pin to use an internal pull-down resistor, so it stays at 0V. Connect one end of the button to the GPIO input pin and the other end to the 3V3 voltage source. When the button is pressed, the GPIO pin is short-circuited with the 3V3 source, so its voltage is drawn up to 3V3 (see Figure 5-9).

- Configure the GPIO pin to use an internal pull-up resistor, so it stays at 3V3. Connect one end of the button to the GPIO input pin and the other end to the ground. When the button is pressed, the GPIO pin is short-circuited with the ground, so its voltage is drawn down to 0V (see Figure 5-10).

In both cases, the GPIO pin will detect a voltage change and trigger the code. For this demonstration, you'll be using option 2. You can add some circuits on top of the LED circuit, as shown in Figure 5-11. The photo is shown in Figure 5-12. You attach one end of the button to GPIO pin 4, which is configured to have a pull-up resistor that keeps it at 3V3. The other end of the button is connected to the ground through a current-limiting resistor. When the button is pressed, the GPIO pin 4 is short-circuited to the ground and should drop to 0V.

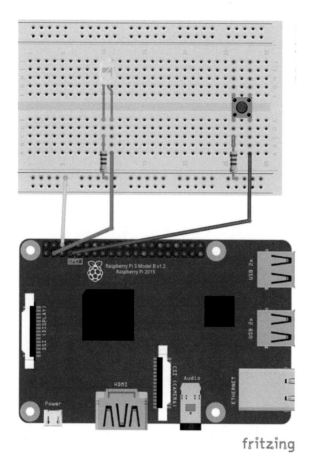

Figure 5-11. *The button circuit diagram (image created with Fritzing)*

Figure 5-12.   *The button circuit*

Then you can write some code to detect the voltage drop and toggle the LED (see Listing 5-4).

Listing 5-4.   Using a Button to Toggle the LED

```rust
extern crate rust_gpiozero;
use rust_gpiozero::*;

fn main() {
    let mut led = LED::new(2);
    let mut button = Button::new(4);
```

```
loop{
    println!("wait for button");
    button.wait_for_press(None);
    // Make the led switch on
    println!("button pressed!");
    led.toggle();
    }
}
```

You first create a LED and a Button. The Button::new() function will configure that pin to what you describe in option 2. If you want to use option 1, you can use Button::new_with_pulldown() instead. In the loop, you called button_wait_for_press(). This will block the program until the button is pressed. You can optionally set a timeout by replacing the None parameter with a Some(f32). The f32 number is the timeout in seconds. When the button is clicked, the function will return and continue to the next line, led.toggle(), which does what its name suggests: toggles the LED's on/off state.

As mentioned before, inside the button, there are two pieces of metal. When you press the button, you might imagine that the two pieces of metal touch each other immediately and stay touched until you let go. But in reality, the metal pieces might bounce off each other after they make contact for a fraction of a second. So there will be a very short period of time when the metal pieces touch and bounce off repeatedly until they finally settle in the touched position. Since the loop runs very fast, the bounce might trigger the button.wait_for_press() function multiple times, so the LED will flicker and might not reach the final state you want it to be.

To counter this issue, you can *debounce* the circuit by only allowing the button press to be triggered once in a short period of time. For example, when the code detects that a button is pressed, it can ignore all the other button press events in the next second. You can improve the button click code, as shown in Listing 5-5.

Listing 5-5. Debouncing the Button

```rust
extern crate rust_gpiozero;
use rust_gpiozero::*;
use std::time::{Duration, Instant};

fn main() {
    let mut led = LED::new(2);
    let mut button = Button::new(4);

    let mut last_clicked = Instant::now();
    loop{
        button.wait_for_press(None);

        if last_clicked.elapsed() < Duration::new(1, 0) {
            continue
        }

        led.toggle();
        last_clicked = Instant::now()
    }
}
```

The last_clicked variable keeps track of when the button is last clicked using std::time::Instant::now(). When the button.wait_for_ press() function returns, you first check last_clicked.elapsed(), which is the time elapsed since you last called Instant::now(). If the elapsed time is less than a second (Duration::new(1, 0))[3], the code considers this press event to be a bounce and ignores it by continuing. Otherwise, it lets it through and toggles the LED, then updates the last_clicked timestamp. With this debounce functionality, the LED no longer flickers. Even if

---

[3]Duration::new() takes two arguments, the first is the seconds and the second argument is the additional nanoseconds. Therefore, (1, 0) means 1 second + 0 nanosecond = 1 second.

you accidentally click the button multiple times in one second, it will be toggled only once. If you think one second is too long, you can reduce the debounce time to make the button more responsive.

Cross-Compiling to Raspberry Pi

You might notice that the Rust program compiles relatively slowly on your Raspberry Pi. This is because the Raspberry Pi CPU is not as powerful as most mainstream desktop CPUs. But Raspberry Pi's CPU is already quite powerful in the embedded world. For some applications, you can expect much weaker (but more energy-efficient) CPUs or even microcontrollers. Those devices are designed to run on very limited CPU, memory, and battery conditions, so it's not possible to load all the source code onto them and compile it on these devices.

This is when you need to use cross-compilation. Cross-compilation means you compile the source code on a different machine (the host) than the one running it (the target). For example, you can compile the code on a powerful, Intel-x86-based Linux desktop and run the binary on the Raspberry Pi target. In this case, the compiler itself is running on an x86 architecture CPU, but it generates machine code (and binary format) for an ARM architecture CPU.

To set up the cross-compilation environment, you need to move back to the Linux desktop/laptop. You can install the compiler toolchain for Raspberry Pi, which runs on the ARM Cortex-A53 CPU. You can add a compile target with `rustup`:

```
rustup target add armv7-unknown-linux-gnueabihf
```

Note   You might be wondering why you install the `armv7` target while the ARM Cortex-A53 CPU is advertised as ARMv8 architecture. This is because the ARM Cortex-A53 CPU supports both 32-bit mode and 64-bit mode. By default, the Raspbian is built on a 32-bit Linux. Therefore, the CPU will run in 32-bit mode, which only supports ARMv7-compatible features. If you run `cat/proc/cpuinfo`, it will also report itself as an ARMv7 CPU.

You also need a linker. You might not be aware of the linker when you work on an x86-based Linux. Most of the time, the linker was already installed when you installed other programs. Usually, the linker comes in the package of a C compiler so you can install gcc (GNU Compiler Collection) to get the ARM linker:

```
sudo apt-get install gcc-5-multilib-arm-linux-gnueabihf
```

Before you compile, you also need to let `cargo` know where to look for the linker. You can open the configuration file called `~/.cargo/config` (create one if it doesn't exist yet) and add the following setting:

```
[target.armv7-unknown-linux-gnueabihf]
linker = "arm-linux-gnueabihf-gcc-5"
```

This means, "when you compile for the target `armv7-unknonw-linux-gnueabihf`, use the linker provided by `arm-linux-gnueabihf-gcc-5`."

Now you'll create a new project with `cargo new blink-cross-compile`. You can open the `src/main.rs` file and copy the code for blinking an LED (see Listing 5-2) into it. Also don't forget to add the `rust_gpiozero` dependency to the `Cargo.toml` file.

To compile the Rust project to a specific target, use the `--target` argument like so:

```
cargo build --target=armv7-unknown-linux-gnueabihf
```

This will produce a binary in target/armv7-unknown-linux-gnueabihf/debug/ named blink-cross-compile. Notice that the binary is placed in the target/armv7-unknown-linux-gnueabihf folder, not in the default target/debug folder. If you try to execute this binary on the x86 Linux system, you'll get the following error message:

```
$ ./blink-cross-compile
bash: ./blink-cross-compile: cannot execute binary file: Exec
format error
```

This is because this binary is cross-compiled for ARM. You can verify this by examining the file with the UNIX file command:

```
$ file ./blink-cross-compile
./blink-cross-compile: ELF 32-bit LSB shared object, ARM, EABI5
version 1 (SYSV),
  dynamically linked, interpreter /lib/ld-, for GNU/Linux 3.2.0,
  BuildID[sha1]=43d4fc4e17539883185e15c3d442986f2fb2f03d, not
  stripped
```

The final step is to copy this binary onto the Raspberry Pi SD card and boot up the Raspbian OS. Once the Raspberry Pi is booted, open a terminal and cd to the location of the binary and execute it. You should see the LED blinking just like before.

How Does the GPIO Code Work?

The rust_gpiozero crate abstracts away most of the complexity of setting up the GPIO pins. But you can take a look at how it works at a lower level.

As mentioned in the section entitled "Controlling the GPIO Pins," the GPIO registers are exposed in two different interfaces: /dev/gpiomem and Sysfs. Sysfs exposes the GPIO registers as virtual devices, which is easier to understand, so I'll start with those.

To achieve the same effect as Listing 5-1 of turning on an LED, you can write a simple shell script using the Sysfs virtual files (see Listing 5-6).

Listing 5-6. Turning On the LED with Sysfs

```
echo "2" > /sys/class/gpio/export
echo "out" > /sys/class/gpio/gpio2/direction

echo "0" > /sys/class/gpio/gpio2/value
```

First, you need to write the pin number to the /sys/class/gpio/ export file. This tells Sysfs that you want to work with the specified pin. Before you export the pin, the virtual pin device /sys/class/gpio/gpio2 does not exist. So you first export the pin 2 with this:

```
echo "2" > /sys/class/gpio/export
```

A new device, called /sys/class/gpio/gpio2, will appear. You can then set the direction of the pin by writing either in or out to the /sys/ class/gpio/gpio2/direction file. Because you are using this pin as an output device, you echo the text out to it. This effectively sets the registers that control the GPIO 2's mode. Then setting the pin to high or low is as simple as writing 1 or 0 to the /sys/class/gpio/gpio2/value file.

These Sysfs files are basically abstractions around the registers that control the GPIO pins. But the rust_gpiozero crate uses a more low-level crate, rppal, to interact with the GPIO pins. For performance reasons, the rppal crate does not use the Sysfs interface. Instead, it works with the / dev/gpiomem directly. The /dev/gpiomem is a virtual device that represents the memory-mapped GPIO registers. If you call the mmap() system call on /dev/gpiomem, the GPIO registers will be mapped to the designated virtual memory addresses. You can then read or write the bits in memory to control the registers directly.

> **Tip**   The /dev/gpiomem virtual device was created to overcome
> the permission issue. Before /dev/gpiomem was available, you
> could access the GPIO-related memory address with /dev/mem.
> However, /dev/mem exposes the whole system memory and requires
> root permission to access. But since GPIO access is so common
> on Raspberry Pi, every program that interacts with GPIO needs to
> use root access, which creates a security hazard. Therefore, /dev/
> gpiomem was created to expose only the GPIO-related part of the
> memory with no special permission needed. In the rppal source
> code, you can see it tries /dev/gpiomem first. If any error occurs, it
> falls back to /dev/mem but then requires root access.

If you look into rppal's source code, you can see that it uses the unsafe
code block to mmap() the /dev/gpiomem device. Once this device is mapped
into the virtual memory, you can write bits to set the direction and value
of the pins with low-level memory manipulation. Listing 5-7 shows the
relevant part of the code from rppal's textsrc/gpio/mem.rs file.

Listing 5-7. The Code in rppal that Manipulates GPIO

```rust
const PATH_DEV_GPIOMEM: &str = "/dev/gpiomem";

const GPFSEL0: usize = 0x00;
const GPSET0: usize = 0x1c / std::mem::size_of::<u32>();
const GPCLR0: usize = 0x28 / std::mem::size_of::<u32>();
const GPLEV0: usize = 0x34 / std::mem::size_of::<u32>();

pub struct GpioMem {}

impl GpioMem {
    // ...
    fn map_devgpiomem() -> Result<*mut u32> {
```

```rust
        // ...
        // Memory-map /dev/gpiomem at offset 0
        let gpiomem_ptr = unsafe {
            libc::mmap(
                ptr::null_mut(),
                GPIO_MEM_SIZE,
                PROT_READ | PROT_WRITE,
                MAP_SHARED,
                gpiomem_file.as_raw_fd(),
                0,
            )
        };

        Ok(gpiomem_ptr as *mut  u32)
    }
    #[inline(always)]
    fn write(&self, offset: usize, value: u32) {
        unsafe {
            ptr::write_volatile(self.mem_ptr.add(offset), value);
        }
    }

    #[inline(always)]
    pub(crate) fn set_high(&self, pin: u8) {
        let offset = GPSET0 + pin as usize / 32;
        let shift = pin % 32;
        self.write(offset, 1 << shift);
    }

    #[inline(always)]
    pub(crate) fn set_low(&self, pin: u8) {
        let offset = GPCLR0 + pin as usize / 32;
```

```rust
    let shift = pin % 32;
    self.write(offset, 1 << shift);
}

pub(crate) fn set_mode(&self, pin: u8, mode: Mode) {
    let offset = GPFSEL0 + pin as usize / 10;
    let shift = (pin % 10) * 3;

    // ...

    let reg_value = self.read(offset);
    self.write(
        offset,
        (reg_value & !(0b111 << shift)) |
            ((mode as u32) << shift),
    );
}
}
```

I won't go into detail here, but you can see the `libc::mmap()` call inside the `map_devgpiomem()` function. You can also see that all the operations you used have corresponding functions in them:

- Set direction: `set_mode()`
- Set pin to high: `set_high()`
- Set pin to low: `set_low()`

All these functions write directly to memory with `std::mem::transmute()` inside `unsafe` blocks. You might wonder how do they know which memory address is for which functionality? They are all defined in the manual of the Broadcom BCM2837B0 chip.

Where Do You Go from Here?

This chapter only scratched the surface of physical computing with Rust, or programming for embedded systems in a general sense. There are many directions you can go to explore this field further. As usual, there is an "Are We X Yet?" page for embedded systems in Rust: Are We Embedded Yet? (`https://afonso360.github.io/rust-embedded/`), where you can find exciting progress of the embedded ecosystem.

In Rust's core team, there are some domain-specific working groups. The Embedded Devices Working Group is responsible for overseeing the Rust embedded ecosystem. They also maintain a curated list of exciting projects and resources at `https://github.com/rust-embedded/awesome-embedded-rust`. If you want to follow the latest development and the working group's future direction, you might want to follow the issues on their coordination repository: `https://github.com/rust-embedded/wg`.

There are a few directions you can explore. The first is to build on top of Raspberry Pi. This chapter only discussed LED and buttons, but there are lots of other hardware you can connect to it. For example:

- Buzzers

- Light sensors

- Sound sensors

- Orientation sensors

- Cameras

- Humidity and temperature sensors

- Infrared sensors

- Ultrasonic sensors

- Touch screens

- Servo motors

There are also add-on boards called "HATs" (Hardware Attached on Top). These are boards with a lot of the hardware components packed into one. They are designed in a way that they can mount directly on top of the Raspberry Pi board and connect with its GPIO pins. The board will also communicate with the Raspberry Pi board and configure the GPIO pins for you. This provides an easy way to try many different kinds of hardware without worrying about wiring on a breadboard. You can find crates like sensehat, which provides an abstraction layer for a specific HAT called the *Sense HAT*. There is also a tutorial accompanying the crate: https://github.com/thejpster/pi-workshop-rs/.

You can also explore other boards and platforms. Rust supports many different computer architectures, so there are many boards available. For instance, the Embedded Working Group published *The Embedded Rust Book*[4]. In the book, they teach you how to program a STM32F3DISCOVERY board, which runs an STM32F303VCT6 microcontroller. Many of the tutorials are using the QEMU emulator, so you don't need actual hardware to get started. You can build your code and run it on a hardware emulator.

You can also go deeper. One thing that the chapter doesn't mention is how to run Rust on a bare-metal environment. Bare metal means the Rust program runs directly on the hardware without an operating system. In such a case, you can't use the standard library because many of the standard library functions depend on the platform. Instead, you need to set the #![no_std] attribute on the crate to let the Rust compiler know that you can't use libstd. It will then use libcore, which is a platform-agnostic subset of libstd. This will also exclude many features you might not want in an embedded environment, like dynamic memory allocation and runtime. *The Embedded Rust Book* will get you started with bare-metal programming. If you are looking to go deeper, you can read the advanced book, *The Embedonomicon*[5]. You might want to go even further and build your own operating system, but Chapter 7 also touches on that topic.

---

[4]https://rust-embedded.github.io/book/intro/index.html
[5]https://docs.rust-embedded.org/embedonomicon/index.html

CHAPTER 6

Artificial Intelligence and Machine Learning

What Is Machine Learning?

Artificial intelligence and machine learning have always been hot topics in news and science fiction. Recently they got more media attention because of technology breakthroughs in deep learning and more consumer-facing applications on the market. The terms *machine learning* and *artificial intelligence* are sometimes used interchangeably, but there is a subtle difference. Artificial intelligence focuses on "intelligence". An AI system tries to behave as if it possesses human intelligence, no matter what the underlying method or algorithm is. But in machine learning, the focus is on "learning," where the system is trying to learn something from the data without a human explicitly programming the knowledge. For example, one of the early successes in AI was the expert system. In an expert system, the knowledge of a particular field is written down as rules and programmed directly into the code, so the system can answer questions or perform tasks as if it were a domain expert. This kind of system might appear to have some level of human intelligence, but underneath it's not actually "learning" from data. So this system can be called an AI system but not a machine learning system.

Researchers tried many different strategies to build AI systems, not necessarily machine learning. But machine learning gets its popularity

© Shing Lyu 2020
S. Lyu, *Practical Rust Projects*, https://doi.org/10.1007/978-1-4842-5599-5_6

due to a few technical advancements. First, the computing power of modern CPUs and GPUs have grown exponentially because of innovations in hardware technology. This means that machine learning models can finally be trained in a reasonable time. The rise of the Internet also led to more and more data can be collected at very low cost, so you finally have enough data to power machine learning algorithms that require a large amount of data, like deep neural networks. All these factors have contributed to the boom of machine learning in the recent decade.

Supervised vs. Unsupervised Learning

There are two main branches of machine learning: supervised versus unsupervised learning. In a supervised learning setting, you give the algorithm a fully-labeled training dataset. For example, if you are trying to distinguish cat pictures from dog pictures, you need to prepare a large number of photos with the label "cat" or "dog". Because the algorithm can check its prediction with the label (or sometimes referred to as the "ground-truth"), the algorithm can learn from its errors and improve its predictions.

But a fully-labeled dataset is not always available. Unless there is an automated way of collecting the label with 100% accuracy, you have to fall back to label them manually. This takes tremendous time and money. Even if the data can be collected automatically, the quality of the data might not be ideal because of noise. Therefore, when getting a high-quality fully-labeled dataset is not possible, you can only rely on an unsupervised learning algorithm to do the job. An unsupervised algorithm takes a training dataset without labels and tries to learn the patterns from the data itself. For example, if you want to distinguish between flower species, you can let the algorithm group the flowers by their color, shape, leaf shape, etc. But without ground-truth labels to check against, one algorithm might focus on the color and put a white rose into the same category as a white lily. Another algorithm might focus on the shape and categorize roses of all colors into one group. So unsupervised learning usually performs poorer or is less predictable than a supervised model, but it's still very useful when labeled training data is hard to come by.

There are other categories of machine learning, like *semi-supervised learning*, which uses a partially-labeled dataset to get high accuracy with a low dataset preparation cost. There is also *reinforced learning*, which takes feedback from the environment to correct future behavior. For example, a maze-navigating robot can get a reward every time it successfully reaches the end of a maze. It can learn the way to navigate a maze by seeking maximum reward and avoiding potential penalties. This chapter focusing on supervised learning and unsupervised learning.

What Are You Building?

This section uses two examples to illustrate supervised and unsupervised learning. It starts with unsupervised learning. The code for unsupervised learning is simpler than supervised learning so you can get a taste of a machine learning program without being overwhelmed by the details. You'll be building a model that can distinguish different cat breeds.

The model collected body size measurements from three cat breeds: Persian, British Shorthair, and Ragdoll (see Figures 6-1 to 6-3). Since these three breeds have slightly different body heights and lengths, you can run a K-means clustering model (explained in the section titled "Clustering Cat Breeds with K-Means") on these two features. The model, once trained, can be used to cluster cats into different breeds automatically. Because K-means can only see the similarity between the data points, it can group the cats into groups but it can't tell exactly which group is which cat breed.

Figure 6-1. *Persian cat*

Figure 6-2. *British shorthair cat*

Figure 6-3. *Ragdoll cat*

190

The second example is for supervised learning. Similar to the previous model, you have a handful of body measurements, but this time from both cats and dogs. There are labels that indicate if each body measurement is taken from a cat or a dog. Using this dataset, you'll use a neural network model to learn how to tell a cat from a dog. In machine learning, this kind of job is called a *classification* problem. When the model is trained, it can predict if a given body measurement belongs to a cat or dog, even if the data is not part of the training set. For simplicity's sake, you'll use only the height and body length as the input.

These machine learning models don't exist in a vacuum. Besides training the model and using the model, there are many tasks involved, like data preparation, cleaning, and visualization. You'll also learn how to use Rust to generate artificial training data, writing and reading the data as CSV (comma-separated values) files, and visualizing the data. The demo programs consist of a few loosely-related binary executables. They will not communicate directly but through passing CSV files. This way, it minimizes the dependency between the steps.

Introducing the rusty-machine Crate

The machine learning ecosystem in any programming language relies on a strong foundation. Building machine learning libraries involves not only the machine learning algorithm itself, but also many fundamental operations like numerical computing, linear algebra, statistics, and data manipulation.

This chapter uses the `rusty-machine` crate. The `rusty-machine` crate contains many traditional machine learning algorithms implemented in Rust. Although deep learning is the hottest topic in machine learning now, there are no mature Rust-based libraries yet. Most of the deep learning libraries in Rust are bindings to libraries in other languages, so the API design is not very Rusty. Deep learning models are also harder to understand by intuition because they involve more advanced mathematical theories, which might be a distraction from the code architecture and the Rust API.

Some of the machine learning algorithms that `rusty-machine` contains are:

- Linear regression

- Logistic regression

- Generalized linear models

- K-means clustering*

- Neural networks*

- Gaussian process regression

- Support vector machines

- Gaussian mixture models

- Naive Bayes classifiers

- DBSCAN

- K-nearest neighbor classifiers

- Principal component analysis

It uses the `rulinalg` crate for linear algebra. Part of the `rulinalg` crate is re-exported in the `rusty_machine::linalg` namespace, so you don't need to import `rulinalg` manually. It also contains useful data transformation tools for data pre-processing, which you'll use later for normalization.

Clustering Cat Breeds with K-Means
Introduction to the K-Means Algorithm

You don't need to be a cat expert to identify different cat breeds. A Persian cat looks different from a British Shorthair in many aspects: their coat has a different length, their face looks different, and their average size is also different. Categorizing things is a human trait that helps us make sense of this world. But machines don't have such an instinct, so we need to program the power of mathematics into them. This kind of problem is called the *clustering* problem, and a popular algorithm to solve this problem is *K-means*.

Since this is a book for general Rust enthusiasts, not mathematicians, I am going to explain the concept in plain English. You can easily find the formal mathematical definitions by searching "K-means" online.

The concept of K-means is simple. To cluster the points into k groups, you want to split them in a way that the points in a group are close to each other, but far from points in other groups. The exact steps to do this are:

1. Randomly assign k points as the "centroids". The centroids are the center points of each cluster.

2. Assignment: For all the other points, assign them to the group of the nearest centroids.

3. Update the centroids: For each group, find the center point (i.e., the mean) of all the points in the group and use this center point as the new centroid.

4. Repeat Steps 2 and 3 until the centroids no longer move.

As you can imagine, during each update, the centroids will move toward the center of the points "cloud," and during the next assignment, some points might be assigned to a new centroid because the centroid position changed. You continue this process until the centroids no longer move; this is when you say the model *converges*. You can see a graphical example in Figure 6-4.

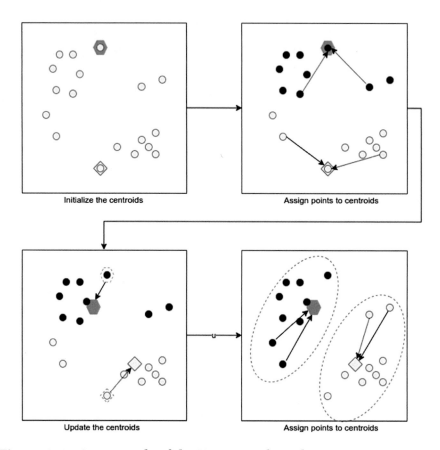

Figure 6-4. *An example of the K-means algorithm*

In practice, the initial location of the centroids matters a lot to the final result. If you assign the initial centroids poorly, the algorithm might converge to a result that is not ideal[1]. It might also take longer for

---

[1]In mathematics, we say it converges to a local optimum, rather than the global optimum.

the model to converge. You can use an algorithm called K-means++ to initialize the initial centroids better. The intuition behind it is that you want to spread out the initial centroids as far as possible. The exact steps to do this are as follows:

1. Choose the first centroid randomly from all the points.

2. For each point x, calculate the distance to its nearest existing centroid as $D(x)$.

3. To find the next centroid, pick a point with a probability proportional to $D(x)^2$. What this means is that if a point x is farther away from any existing centroids, its $D(x)$ is larger, and it has a higher probability to be chosen as a new centroid.

4. Repeat Steps 2 and 3 until all the centroids are picked.

By using the K-means++ algorithm, the initial centroids are spread out as far away from each other as possible. This will usually result in a better result. This is the default initialization method used by `rusty-machine`.

The Training Data

To prepare the training data, you need to collect body measurements from many cats. Since this is time-consuming, and you probably don't want to get scratches and bites from grumpy cats, this example uses a fake dataset using the averages. You can generate some artificial cat body measurements with a normal distribution centered on the average. The body measurements are:

- Height: The height from the ground to a cat's shoulder

- Length: The length from a cat's head to its bottom, excluding the tail

The average measurements of the three breeds are:

- Persian: Height 22.5 cm, length 40.5 cm

- British Shorthair: Height 38.0 cm, length 50.0 cm

- Ragdoll: Height 25.5 cm, length 48.0 cm

To have a fair amount of data points for demonstration, there are 2,000 samples per cat breed. These data points are generated using a normal distribution around the average with an arbitrarily chosen standard deviation of 1.8 cm. This standard deviation creates a nice cloud of data points with a little overlap, which will help illustrate how K-means works.

To generate this training data, you are going to set up `rusty-machine` so that you can use the linear algebra part. First, let's create a Rust project with `cargo new cat-breeds-k-means`. In the `Cargo.toml` file, you need to add `rusty-machine`, `rand` (for random number generation), and `rand_distr` (for common probability distributions like normal distribution).

Listing 6-1. Adding Dependencies to Cargo.toml

```
[dependencies]
rusty-machine = "0.5.4"
rand = "0.7.0"
rand_distr = "0.2.1"
```

Because you are going to have multiple binaries in this project, you can't simply have a `src/main.rs` and run it with `cargo run`. Cargo has support for multiple binaries in a project. Simply add the files to `src/bin/`, for example `src/bin/generate.rs`. Then you can run it with `cargo run --bin generate`.

In the `src/bin/generate.rs` file, you can start by declaring the crates you are using:

```
extern crate rusty_machine;
extern crate rand;
```

You want to build a function that can generate training data around the given average with the normal distribution. So you first define its function signature, as shown in Listing 6-2.

Listing 6-2. Function Signature for generate_data

```
fn generate_data(centroids: &Matrix<f64>,
                 points_per_centroid: usize,
                 noise: f64)
    -> Matrix<f64> { ... }
```

As you can see in Listing 6-2, the function takes three parameters:

- A matrix[2] of f64 values. Each row is the average height and length of a cat breed. It should have a shape of (3×2) (three cat breeds × two dimensions—height and length—per breed).

- The number of data points you want to generate for each cat breed.

- The standard deviation used for the normal distribution, a.k.a. the noise.

The return value will be a matrix containing all the generated data points. It should have the shape (the total number of samples × 2).

The logic is pretty simple; you have nested for loops that iterate through the three centroids and generate the required number of samples for each centroid. This is shown in Listing 6-3.

---

[2]Matrix is provided by the rulinalg crate wrapped in rusty-machine.

Listing 6-3. Function to Generate the Samples

```
extern crate rusty_machine;
extern crate rand;

use rusty_machine::linalg::{Matrix, BaseMatrix};

use rand::thread_rng;
use rand::distributions::Distribution; // for using .sample()
use rand_distr::Normal; // split from rand since 0.7
use std::io;
use std::vec::Vec;

fn generate_data(centroids: &Matrix<f64>,
                 points_per_centroid: usize,
                 noise: f64)
    -> Matrix<f64> {
    assert!(centroids.cols() > 0, "centroids cannot be empty.");
    assert!(centroids.rows() > 0, "centroids cannot be empty.");
    assert!(noise >= 0f64, "noise must be non-negative.");
    let mut raw_cluster_data =
        Vec::with_capacity(centroids.rows() *
            points_per_centroid * centroids.cols());

    let mut rng = thread_rng(); // [1]
    let normal_rv = Normal::new(0f64, noise).unwrap(); // [2]

    for _ in 0..points_per_centroid { // [3]
        // generate points from each centroid
        for centroid in centroids.iter_rows() {
            // generate a point randomly around the centroid
            let mut point = Vec::with_capacity(centroids.cols());
            for feature in centroid.iter() {
                point.push(feature + normal_rv.sample(&mut rng));
            }
```

```
        // push point to raw_cluster_data
        raw_cluster_data.extend(point);
    }
}

Matrix::new(centroids.rows() * points_per_centroid,
            centroids.cols(),
            raw_cluster_data)
}
```

When you first enter the function, you validate that the centroids matrix is not empty, and the standard deviation is non-negative. Then you initialize a raw_cluster_data vector with the expected capacity. You allocate the memory for the raw_cluster_data in advance, so the vector does not need to resize when it grows. In [1], you create the random number generator from the rand crate. Since you want to generate random numbers with a normal distribution, you need to initialize a normal distribution from rand_distr::Normal ([2]). This normal distribution has a mean (average) of 0 and standard deviation of noise. You can then add this random deviation to the average cat body measurements.

Then comes the actual generation of samples. The outer for loop ([3]) makes sure you repeat the generation *n* times, where *n* is the number of desired samples per centroid. In the inner loop, you iterate through the centroids, so you generate a sample for each. This ensures that you generate a total number of (number of centroids × number of sample per centroid) samples. In this case, you have 3 × 2000 = 6,000 samples.

In the body of the loop, you create a temporary vector of size 2 to hold the height and length. For each dimension, you get a random number from the normal distribution you just initialized. This random number is generated around 0. Then you add the random number to the average height or length, so you'll have samples that follow a normal distribution around the average height or length of the cat breed. Finally, this point is added to the `raw_cluster_data` vector. The vector will then become a large 1D array. If you use the symbol A_h to denote the height of cat A, and A_l for the its length, the `raw_cluster_data` vector for cat A, B, and C will look like this:

$$\left[A_h, A_l, B_h, B_l, C_h, C_l\right]$$

But what you actually want is a matrix of samples, one sample per row:

$$\begin{bmatrix} A_h & A_l \\ B_h & N_l \\ C_h & C_l \end{bmatrix}$$

To convert this, you pass the 1D array to the `Matrix::new()` function. You can provide the desired shape (the number of rows and columns), and `Matrix::new()` will reshape the 1D array into the matrix you want. Finally, you return this matrix as the training data.

Exporting as CSV

In the `main()` function of the `src/bin/generate.rs`, you are going to call the `generate_data()` function and output the data to STDOUT in the CSV format. CSV(comma-separated value) is a simple format for tabular data: the rows are separated into lines, and the columns are separated by commas. This format is supported in most programming languages and spreadsheet software (e.g., LibreOffice Calc and Microsoft Excel).

Although the CSV format is quite simple, it's still too error-prone to format it without the help of a library. I chose to use the `csv` crate to save the trouble. Simply add the line `csv = "1.1"` to the `dependencies` section of the `Cargo.toml`. Then in the `main()` function, you can put everything together, as shown in Listing 6-4.

Listing 6-4. Outputting CSV

```
// settings
const CENTROIDS: [f64;6] = [
    //Height, length
    22.5, 40.5, // Persian
    38.0, 50.0, // British shorthair
    25.5, 48.0, // Ragdoll
];
const NOISE: f64 = 1.8;
const SAMPLES_PER_CENTROID: usize = 2000;

fn generate_data(...) { ... }

fn main() -> Result<(), std::io::Error> {
    let centroids = Matrix::new(3, 2, CENTROIDS.to_vec());

    let samples = generate_data(&centroids,
        SAMPLES_PER_CENTROID, NOISE);

    let mut writer = csv::Writer::from_writer(io::stdout());
    writer.write_record(&["height", "length"])?;
    for sample in samples.iter_rows() {
        writer.serialize(sample)?;
    }
    Ok(())
}
```

First, you convert the centroids from the const CENTROIDS vector into an array. Ideally, all these parameters should be configurable from command-line arguments, but I'll leave that for the next section. For now, you'll just hard-code the configurations as consts at the beginning of the file.

Then you call the generate_data() function and assign the generated training data to the samples variable. To write these samples into CSV format, you need to initialize a `csv::Writer`. For simplicity, you are going to write the CSV directly to STDOUT. You'll see more advanced usage of writing directly to files in the section entitled "Detecting Cats Versus Dogs with the Neural Network". You initialize the `Writer` by:

```
let mut writer = csv::Writer::from_writer(io::stdout());
```

To write a simple plain-text line to the CSV output, you can use `writer.write_record()`. It takes (a reference to) an array of strings. So you write the header "height" and "length" to it. You can also provide a serializable (i.e., implements `serde::Serialize`) struct and let it be automatically converted to a valid CSV line. This can be done by `writer.serialize()`. So you iterate through the rows of the sample array and write each line as CSV by:

```
for sample in samples.iter_rows() {
    writer.serialize(sample)?;
}
```

Now, if you run `cargo run --bin generate`, you'll see 6,001 lines (including a heading line) being printed to the screen. You can easily pipe this to a file by using `cargo run --bin generate > training data.csv`.

Moving the Configuration Into a File

In the previous section, you hard-coded all the configurations as `consts` in the source code. This becomes an impendence when you want to experiment with many different configurations. Building a machine learning application involves a lot of experimentation. You usually need to try many different parameters and settings to get the best result. If you hard-code the parameters in the code, you'll need to change them and re-compile the program every time. It's easier to put those configurations in a configuration file, then specify the configuration file using command-line arguments. This way, you can easily choose a configuration at runtime. Another benefit is that you can keep all the configuration files in the source code repository so that you can reproduce a specific experiment quickly.

There are many machine-readable configuration file formats to choose from. For example, TOML, JSON, YAML, XML, and RON[3]. This example uses TOML because Cargo uses it, so it's widely accepted by the Rust community. Also, it has excellent parser and deserialization support in Rust.

You can move the consts into a file named config/generate.toml (see Listing 6-5). You'll notice that the syntax is slightly different from Rust, but it's still straightforward.

Listing 6-5. The TOML Configuration File

```
centroids = [ # Height, length
    22.5, 40.5, # Persian
    38.0, 50.0, # British short hair
    25.5, 48.0, # Ragdoll
]
noise = 1.8
samples_per_centroid = 2000
```

But the value types in TOML does not map one-to-one to Rust types. How do you make sure the values are parsed into Rust as a [f64;6], f64 and usize? The toml crate, which is the TOML parser you are going to use, can work with serde to deserialize the TOML into a pre-defined Rust

---

[3]The Amethyst framework introduced in Chapter 4 uses RON as its configuration format.

struct. You need to add the toml and serde crates into the dependencies section of your Cargo.toml:

```
[dependencies]
# ...
toml = "0.5.5"
serde = { version = "1.0.103", features = ["derive"] }
```

Then you can define the struct format for the TOML file in the src/bin/generate.rs file (see Listing 6-6).

Listing 6-6. Defining the Config Struct

```
use std::fs::read_to_string;
use serde::Deserialize;
// ...

#[derive(Deserialize)]
struct Config { // [1]
    centroids: [f64;6],
    noise: f64,
    samples_per_centroid: usize,
}

fn main() -> Result<(), std::io::Error> {
    let toml_config_str = read_to_string(
        "config/generate.toml"
    )?; // [2]
    let config: Config = toml::from_str(&toml_config_str)?;
    // ...
}
```

In [1], you derived the serde::Deserialize trait on the Config struct. This will give the toml parser enough information on how to parse the TOML file into the Config struct. Then in [2], you read the config/generate.toml file into a String and pass its reference to `toml::from_str`. Because you set the type of the `config` variable to be `Config`, `toml` will parse it into a `Config` struct using the `Deserialize` implementation. Once it's parsed, you can access the individual fields using dot notation, e.g., `config.centroids`, `config.noise`.

You can then remove all the `const`s and use the `config` instead. For example,

```
let centroids = Matrix::new(3, 2, CENTROIDS.to_vec());
let samples = generate_data(
    &centroids,
    SAMPLES_PER_CENTROID,
    NOISE
);
```

becomes

```
let centroids = Matrix::new(3, 2, config.centroids.to_vec());
let samples = generate_data(
    &centroids,
    config.samples_per_centroid,
    config.noise
);
```

In Listing 6-6, you still hard-codes the path to the TOML file. You can use `StructOpt`, which you learned about in Chapter 2, to make it a command-line parameter. You need to add the `structopt` dependency to `Cargo.toml`:

```
[dependencies]
// ...
structopt = "0.3.5"
```

Then in `src/bin/generate.rs`, you can add an argument called `--config-file` (see Listing 6-7).

Listing 6-7. Adding the --config-file Argument

```
// ...
use structopt::StructOpt;

// ...

#[derive(StructOpt)]
struct Options {
    #[structopt(short = "c", long = "config-file",
                parse(from_os_str))]
    /// Configuration file TOML
    config_file_path: std::path::PathBuf,
}

fn main() -> Result<(), std::io::Error> {
    let options = Options::from_args();
    let toml_config_str = read_to_string(
        options.config_file_path
    )?;
    // ...
}
```

In the `main()` function, you can read the configuration file path dynamically from `Options::from_args()` and pass it to `read_to_string()`. Then to run the generate script, you can use the following command in the shell:

```
cargo run --bin generate -- --config-file config/generate.toml
```

If you want to try different configurations, simply copy-paste the `config/generate.toml`, change some parameters in it, and specify the new filename in the `--config-file` argument. You no longer need to re-compile the `src/bin/generate.rs` script every time you change the configuration. This pattern is also beneficial when you do model training in the following section. One of the key processes in machine learning is parameter selection (or parameter tuning). This involves testing various parameters for the machine learning model to find the best setup. You can test with many different configuration files using this pattern. You can also easily recreate the model with the binary, configuration file, and training data.

Visualizing the Data

Before you jump into learning, it would be nice to see how the data looks. To visualize the training data, you can use a plotting library. Since there is no mature Rust plotting library at the moment, this example uses the popular gnuplot library. Gnuplot is a command-line-driven plotting tool. It's mostly written in C but has a Rust binding.

You need to first install the gnuplot binary by running sudo apt-get install gnuplot in the terminal. Then, you need to add the gnuplot binding crate to the dependencies section of your Cargo.toml:

```
[dependencies]
gnuplot = "0.0.31"
```

Then create a new script in src/bin named plot.rs. The bare minimum code to draw something onto the screen is as simple as Listing 6-8.

Listing 6-8. Minimum Code for Drawing with Gnuplot

```
use std::error::Error;
use gnuplot::{AxesCommon, Caption, Figure};

fn main() -> Result<(), Box<dyn Error>>{

    let mut x: Vec<f64> = Vec::new();
    let mut y: Vec<f64> = Vec::new();

    //TODO: read the CSV data into x and y

    let mut fg = Figure::new();
    fg.axes2d().points(x, y, &[Caption("Cat")]);
```

```
    fg.show();
    Ok(())
}
```

In the main() function of Listing 6-8, you create a gnuplot called Figure. You render a 2D graph using fg.axes2d(), and you draw all the data points onto the 2D canvas using points(). The x and y parameters are vectors holding the x-axis and y-axis coordinates of all the points. You also add a caption "Cat" for the points. To see the figure, run fg.show(), which will open a gnuplot window containing the graph. The graph will look like Figure 6-5.

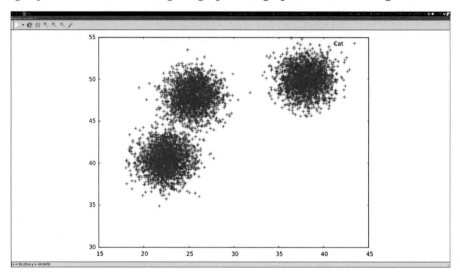

Figure 6-5. *A minimal gnuplot*

One thing you missed in the previous example is how to get the x and y. Since you piped the generated CSV to STDOUT, you can read the data using STDIN. This way, you can easily pipe the CSV generated from the previous section into this plot.rs script:

```
cat training_data.csv | cargo run --bin plot
```

The CSV reading code is very similar to the writing part, just reversing the write with reading (see Listing 6-9).

Listing 6-9. Reading CSV from STDIN

```
// ...
use std::io;

fn main() -> Result<(), Box<dyn Error>>{
    let mut x: Vec<f64> = Vec::new();
    let mut y: Vec<f64> = Vec::new();

    let mut reader = csv::Reader::from_reader(io::stdin());
    for result in reader.records() {
        let record = result?;
        x.push(record[0].parse().unwrap());
        y.push(record[1].parse().unwrap());
    }

    // Drawing the figure

    Ok(())
}
```

First, you create a Reader that reads from io::stdin(). Then you can easily iterate through the rows of the file by using for result in reader. records(). However, the items yielded by the iterator (i.e., the result) have the type of Result<StringRecord, Error>, so you need to get the StringRecord out of the Result with the ? operator:

```
let record = result?;
```

You can access an individual column in a StringRecord using an index like record[0]. This yields a str. Because your x and y requires the type Vec<f64>, you can convert the str to f64 by calling .parse().unwrap(). You push the parsed x and y coordinate values into the x and y vector.

To make the figure easier to understand, you can add titles, a legend, and axes labels to the graph, as shown in Listing 6-10.

Listing 6-10. Adding a Title, Legend, and Labels to the Graph

```
fg.axes2d()
    .set_title("Cat body measurements", &[])
    .set_legend(Graph(0.9), Graph(0.1), &[], &[])
    .set_x_label("height (cm)", &[])
    .set_y_label("length (cm)", &[])
    .points(x, y, &[Caption("Cat")]);
```

Most of the function names are self-explanatory. Only set_legend might look a little confusing. The first two parameters for set_legend are the x and y coordinates of the legend. You set them to 90% of the graph's x width, and 10% of the graph's y height, which is the bottom-right corner of the graph. Most of the functions take some optional flags in an array. This example sticks with the defaults, so you pass empty arrays for the optional parameters. If you rerun the script, the generated figure will look like Figure 6-6.

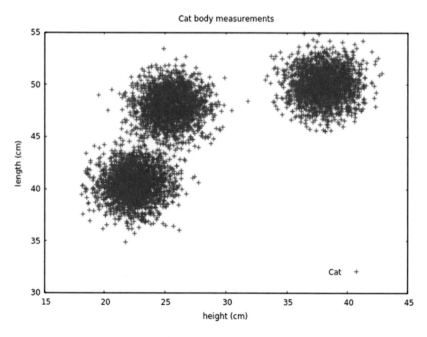

Figure 6-6. *The plot with the title, legend, and axes labels*

Setting Up K-Means

As you can see from Figure 6-6, the cat body measurements form three clusters. You'd expect the K-means algorithm to cluster them into three groups. The K-means model is located in `rusty_machine::learning::k_means::KMeansClassifier`. All of the unsupervised models, including K-means, implement the `rusty_machine::learning::UnSupModel` trait. This trait has a very simple interface, as shown in Listing 6-11.

Listing 6-11. The UnSupModel Trait

```
pub trait UnSupModel<T, U> {
    fn train(&mut self, inputs: &T) -> LearningResult<()>;
    fn predict(&self, inputs: &T) -> LearningResult<U>;
}
```

The `train()` function will take the training data `input` and learn from it. The "knowledge" is stored in the model itself. After the model is trained, you can use the `predict()` function to predict (in this case, cluster) new data based on the knowledge learned from the training data.

Before you can call `train()`, you need to configure the K in the name K-means. K is the number of clusters you expect it to cluster into. From Figure 6-6, you can clearly see there are three clusters. Therefore, you should set $k = 3$. As mentioned in the section titled "What Are You Building?," you create a separate binary for the K-means training and clustering: `src/bin/cluster.rs`. You can start by writing a simple `main()` function, as shown in Listing 6-12.

Listing 6-12. Main Function for Running K-Means Clustering

```
extern crate rusty_machine;

use rusty_machine::learning::k_means::KMeansClassifier;
use rusty_machine::learning::UnSupModel;
```

211

```rust
const CLUSTER_COUNT: usize = 3;

fn main() {
    let samples = read_data_from_stdin().unwrap();

    let mut model = KMeansClassifier::new(CLUSTER_COUNT);
    model.train(&samples).unwrap();

    let classes = model.predict(&samples).unwrap();

    export_result_to_stdout(samples, classes.into_vec()).unwrap();
}
```

The steps in the main() function are pretty straightforward. You load the CSV data from STDIN using a helper function called read_data_from_ stdin(), which I'll discuss soon. You initialize a KMeansClassifier with the configuration K = CLUSTER_COUNT. Then you do model.train() and model.predict() for the same data. The model.train() step will preform the clustering and store the centroids in the model, then model.predict() will return the cluster ID label (i.e., the cat breed) for each data point. You then write the result to STDOUT using another helper function, called export_result_to_stdout(). That's all you need to train a complicated mathematical model in Rust!

The helper functions for reading and outputting data are similar to the ones you saw in the generation and visualization script. The read_data_ from_stdin() function (see Listing 6-13) is almost the same as the plot. rs function (Listing 6-9), except that you convert the output to a Matrix. This is because the KMeansClassifier.train() expects a Matrix, while gnuplot expects a Vec.

Listing 6-13. Reading Data for Training from STDIN

```rust
fn read_data_from_stdin() -> Result<Matrix<f64>, Box<dyn Error>> {
    let mut reader = csv::Reader::from_reader(io::stdin());
    let mut data: Vec<f64>= vec!();
    for result in reader.records() {
        let record = result?;
        data.push(record[0].parse().unwrap());
        data.push(record[1].parse().unwrap());
    }

    Ok(Matrix::new(&data.len() / 2, 2, data))
}
```

The output function export_results_to_stdout() is also a simple call to a csv::Writer (see Listing 6-14). The key to this function is that you want to output the original 2D body measurement data along with the classes data from the clustering result. Imagine you have three cats like so:

$$\begin{bmatrix} 22.5 & 40.5 \\ 38.0 & 50.0 \\ 25.5 & 48.0 \end{bmatrix}$$

They are clustered into class 0, 1, and 2[4], respectively:

$$\begin{bmatrix} 0 \\ 1 \\ 2 \end{bmatrix}$$

---

[4]The class IDs are arbitrary integers; they are categorical, so the number doesn't convey any mathematical meaning.

You want the output CSV to be the two matrixes "stitched" together:

$$\begin{bmatrix} 22.5 & 40.5 & 0 \\ 38.0 & 50.0 & 1 \\ 25.5 & 48.0 & 2 \end{bmatrix}$$

This is achieved by the line `samples.iter_rows().zip(classes)`. The `.zip()` function does exactly the stitching you want.

Listing 6-14. Export the Height and Length Data Together with the Classes as CSV

```
fn export_result_to_stdout(samples: Matrix<f64>,
    classes: Vec<usize>) -> Result<(), Box<dyn Error>> {
    let mut writer = csv::Writer::from_writer(io::stdout());
    writer.write_record(&["height", "length", "class"])?;
    for sample in samples.iter_rows().zip(classes) {
        writer.serialize(sample)?;
    }
    Ok(())
}
```

You export the result to a CSV file for visualization:

```
cat training_data.csv | cargo run --bin cluster > results.csv
```

To make it clear which point belongs to which class, you can use different point symbols and colors for different classes. You can tweak the original visualization script into Listing 6-15.

Listing 6-15. Visualizing the Classes from the K-Means Classification

```rust
use std::error::Error;
use std::io;
use gnuplot::{Figure, Caption, Graph, Color, PointSymbol};
use gnuplot::AxesCommon;

fn main() -> Result<(), Box<dyn Error>>{
    let mut x: [Vec<f64>; 3] =
        [Vec::new(), Vec::new(), Vec::new()];

    let mut y: [Vec<f64>; 3] =
        [Vec::new(), Vec::new(), Vec::new()];
    let mut reader = csv::Reader::from_reader(io::stdin());
    for result in reader.records() {
        let record = result?;
        let class:usize = record[2].parse().unwrap();
        x[class].push(record[0].parse().unwrap());
        y[class].push(record[1].parse().unwrap());
    }

    let mut fg = Figure::new();
    fg.axes2d()
            .set_title("Cat breed classification result", &[])
            .set_legend(Graph(0.9), Graph(0.1), &[], &[])
            .set_x_label("height (cm)", &[])
            .set_y_label("length (cm)", &[])
            .points(
                &x[0],
                &y[0],
                &[Caption("Cat breed 1"), Color("red"),
                PointSymbol('+')],
            )
```

```
                .points(
                        &x[1],
                        &y[1],
                        &[Caption("Cat breed 2"), Color("green"),
                        PointSymbol('x')],
                )
                .points(
                        &x[2],
                        &y[2],
                        &[Caption("Cat breed 3"), Color("blue"),
                        PointSymbol('o')],
                );
        fg.show();
        Ok(())
}
```

Most of the code is the same as in Listing 6-8. However, this time, the x and y is a nested array of three individual arrays. Each sub-array contains the x (or y) coordinates for a specific cluster. For example, x[0] contains the x coordinates of the cat cluster 0, x[1] is for cluster 1, and x[2] is for cluster 2.

To plot the points using different symbols and colors, you use some optional parameters for the text:

- Caption("Cat breed 1") sets the caption for that cluster of points.

- Color("red") sets the point color to red.

- PointSymbol("+") represents the point as a + symbol, so it's easier to distinguish when the graph is printed in black and white.

This results in Figure 6-7.

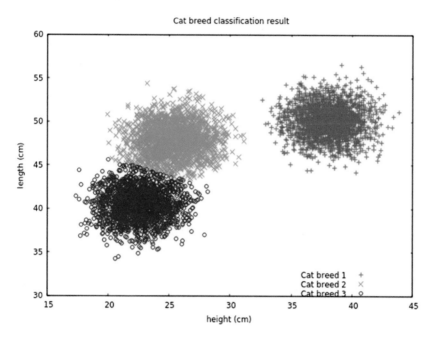

Figure 6-7. *Clustering result for the K-means algorithm*

If you zoom in to the border between the breed 2 (x) and breed 3 (o),
you can see the points are almost split by a straight line (see Figure 6-8).
You know that a normal distribution will probably not look like this. Some
of the breed 2 points might fall in the breed 3 "cloud" and vice versa.
But this is an inherited limitation of K-means. Given only the height and
length, but without a proper ground-truth tagging, the algorithm can only
predict based on the nearest mean (i.e., centroid), resulting in a seemingly
clear-cut line between the clusters.

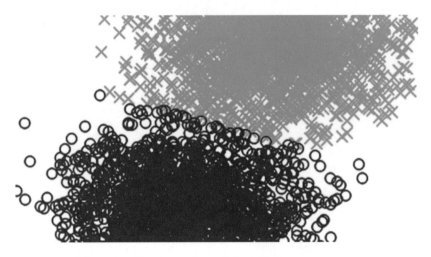

Figure 6-8. *Clear cut between breed 2 and 3*

Detecting Cats versus Dogs with the Neural Network

Introduction to Neural Networks

You've seen how unsupervised models work, so now it's time to shift your attention to a supervised model. The supervised model you are going to use is the Artificial Neural Network (ANN) model or Neural Network for short. Neural Network draws its inspiration from how a human brain works. The human brain consists of neurons. Each neuron takes stimuli and decides if it should be "activated" or not. An activated neuron will send an electrical signal to other connected neurons. So if you have a big network of interconnected neurons, they can learn to react to different inputs by adjusting the way they connect, and how sensitive they are to the stimuli.

Modern neural network models maintain the same guiding principle, but they focus more on solving empirical questions using data, rather than trying to model a human brain accurately. One of the key components of a neural network model is the neuron (or sometimes called a *node*; shown in Figure 6-9). A node consists of one or more inputs (x_i), their weights (w_i), an input function, and an activation function[5]. The input function takes the weighted sum of all the inputs and passes it to the activation function. The weights are adjusted during the learning process to amplify or dampen signals according to the significance of the input signal to the things you want to learn. The result of the input function will be passed to the activation function to determine if the node should be activated or not.

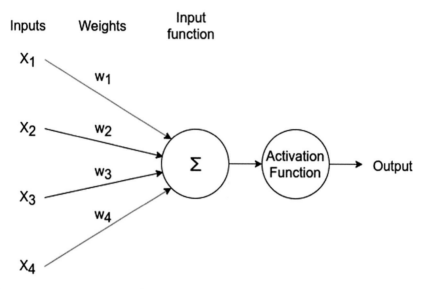

Figure 6-9. *Structure of a neuron/node*

The nodes need to be combined into a network. A simple example is Figure 6-10, which contains two input nodes, two nodes in the middle layer, and one output node. For the dog-or-cat example, you can send the height and length value to the two input nodes, and the output node should give you a signal to indicate if the input data belongs to a dog or cat.

---

[5]rusty-machine uses the Sigmoid function by default.

Each node will determine if it should be activated based on the input it got from the previous stage, combined by the weights.

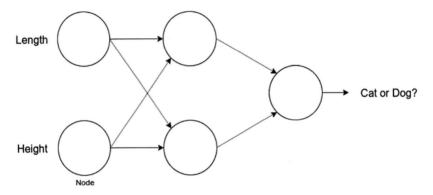

Figure 6-10. *A simple neural network*

In the beginning, you can randomly set the weights, but this won't give any better results than merely guessing. To learn from the training data, you need to adjust the weights in the nodes according to the training data. Because you have the ground-truth answer, you can compare the output of the neural network with the ground-truth; if the output is far off, that means you need to adjust the weights to make a better prediction next time.

You evaluate how good (or bad) the model is currently performing through a loss function. The `rusty-machine` default is the *Binary Cross-Entropy* loss function, which will give a higher value if the output (cat or dog) does not match the ground-truth and a lower value, vice versa. The goal is to adjust the weights to minimize the loss (i.e., make the loss function return the smallest value possible). To achieve this, you use an algorithm called *gradient descent*. Gradient descent will adjust the weight toward the direction by which the loss will go down.

So if you provide a lot of data to the neural network, it will feed a small batch of data into the network and check the network's output against the ground-truth answer. Then it will try to adjust the weights to make the loss go down. Then it will feed the next batch of data and continue to adjust the weights. Once all the data is fed, the neural network should have nodes with weights that capture the characteristics of the training data. When you get a new body measurement, you can feed it to the network. The output will then tell you if the body measurement belongs to a dog or cat

Preparing the Training and Testing Data

To keep the example simple, you are going to use the same kind of input as the K-means example: height and length. You'll create 2,000 samples for cats and 2,000 for dogs. But there is some difference between this data and the K-means data:

- You need to provide the "answer," or the ground-truth labels for each sample.

- You need to generate two sets of data: The training data and testing data.

The reason that you need the ground-truth labels is that a neural network is a supervised model, which means that it needs to learn by comparing its prediction with the ground-truth and trying to improve its accuracy.

You also need to split the data into a training set and a testing set. The training set is used to train the model. The testing set is used to verify how accurate the trained model is. One key point is that the model should never see the data in the testing set during the training phase. The reason is that since you have the answer already, you can't let the model see the testing data during training. Otherwise, it already knows the answer and can quickly achieve 100% accuracy by memorizing the training data.

Even if the algorithm doesn't intentionally memorize the answer, using the testing data in training will usually lead to overfitting. Overfitting is when the model tries to accommodate the particular training dataset too much and fails to generate a model that is general enough. That means the model will work very well on the same set of training data but will fail miserably for any data that it hasn't seen before. Therefore you need to split the data into two sets.

To generate the training data, the overall code structure looks the same as in Listing 6-4. The only difference is in the generate_data() function, presented in Listing 6-16.

Listing 6-16. Sample Generation Function for the Supervised Neural Network Model

```
use serde::Serialize;

#[derive(Debug, Serialize)]
struct Sample { // [1]
    height: f64,
    length: f64,
    category_id: usize
}

fn generate_data(centroids: &Matrix<f64>,
                 points_per_centroid: usize,
                 noise: f64)
    -> Vec<Sample> { // [2]
    // input validation
    let mut samples = Vec::with_capacity(points_per_centroid);

    let mut rng = thread_rng();
    let normal_rv = Normal::new(0f64, noise).unwrap();

    for _ in 0..points_per_centroid {
        // Generate points from each centroid
        for (centroid_id, centroid) in
            centroids.iter_rows().enumerate() {
            let mut point = Vec::with_capacity(centroids.cols());
```

```
        for feature in centroid.iter() {
            point.push(feature + normal_rv.sample(&mut rng));
        }

        samples.push(Sample { // [3]
            height: point[0],
            length: point[1],
            category_id: centroid_id,
        });
    }
}

    samples
}
```

Each row in the new data now has three columns: length, height, and the cat-or-dog label. The cat-or-dog label will be an integer—0 represents dog, and 1 represents cat[6]. You can serialize all the fields into f64, but the integer label will become 0.0 or 1.0 in the CSV file. To force it to serialize to a nice looking 0 or 1, you need to define the "schema". The schema is simply a struct that implements the serde::Serialize trait. You define this in the struct Sample ([1]). The generate data() function will return a Vec<Sample> instead of a Matrix<f64>. When you call csv::Writer. serialize() with a Sample, it will use Serde to serialize it to something like 25.24, 60.03, 1.

You'll create a binary called src/bin/generate_data.rs to generate the training and testing data by running it twice. It generates a total of 4,000 training samples and 4,000 testing samples.

---

[6]This number is assigned arbitrarily. There is no special meaning behind the numbers.

Setting Up the Neural Network Model

After the training and testing data is generated, you need to build the model training and predicting code. You are going to put them in a new binary, called src/bin/train_and_predict.rs. This binary then:

- Reads and parses the training data into a Vec, and shapes it into a Matrix.

- Normalizes the training data.

- Initializes the neural network model.

- Feeds the normalized training data into the model for training.

- Reads and parses the testing data into a Vec, and shapes it into a Matrix.

- Normalizes the testing data using the same parameter for normalizing the training data.

- Uses the trained model to make predictions on the testing data.

I'll discuss each task in the following sections.

Reading the Training and Testing Data

In the K-means example (see Listing 6-13), you read the CSV input from STDIN. However, in a supervised model, you need two input files: the training and testing data. So this time, you are going to give the CSV file paths as CLI arguments and read them directly from the file. Using StructOpt, which was introduced in Chapter 2, you'll create two arguments, called training_data_csv and testing_data_csv (see Listing 6-17).

Listing 6-17. CLI Options for Reading the Training and Testing
CSV File

```rust
use structopt::StructOpt;

#[derive(StructOpt)]
struct Options {
    #[structopt(short = "r", long = "train", parse(from_os_str))]
    /// Training data CSV file
    training_data_csv: std::path::PathBuf,

    #[structopt(short = "t", long = "test", parse(from_os_str))]
    /// Testing data CSV file
    testing_data_csv: std::path::PathBuf,
}

fn main() -> Result<(), Box<dyn Error>>{

    let options = Options::from_args();

    // ...

    Ok(())
}
```

You might recall that you learned how to serialize the data from a Rust
struct into CSV in the section entitled "Detecting Cats Versus Dogs with
the Neural Network". Now you need to do the opposite: to deserialize the
CSV data back to Rust structs. For this, you need to define the same data
schema in a Rust struct and provide it to csv::Reader (see Listing 6-18).

Listing 6-18. Reading the Training Data

```
extern crate rusty_machine;

use serde::Deserialize;
use csv;

use rusty_machine::linalg::Matrix;

#[derive(Debug, Deserialize)]
struct SampleRow { // [1]
    height: f64,
    length: f64,
    category_id: usize,
}

fn read_data_from_csv(file_path: std::path::PathBuf)
    -> Result<(Matrix<f64>, Matrix<f64>), Box<dyn Error>> {
    let mut input_data = vec![];
    let mut label_data = vec![];
    let mut sample_count = 0;
    let mut reader = csv::Reader::from_path(file_path)?; // [2]
    for raw_row in reader.deserialize() { // [3]
        let row: SampleRow = raw_row?;
        input_data.push(row.height);
        input_data.push(row.length);
        label_data.push(row.category_id as f64);
        sample_count += 1
    }

    let inputs = Matrix::new(sample_count, 2, input_data);
    let targets = Matrix::new(sample_count, 1, label_data);
    return Ok((inputs, targets))
}
```

```
fn main() -> Result<(), Box<dyn Error>>{
    let options = Options::from_args();

    let (inputs, targets) = read_data_from_csv(
        options.training_data_csv
    ).unwrap();
    // ...
}
```

The schema you define is the struct SampleRow ([1]), exactly the same as in generate_data.rs. But this time, you derive the Deserialize trait on it. You created a utility function read_data_from_csv() to read the data from CSV file path. The line that actually reads the CSV file is on [2], where you use csv::Reader::from_path(). The path parameter is the PathBuf you get from the CLI options. Once the file is loaded into memory, you loop through the rows obtained by calling reader.deserialize() ([3]). This will deserialize the CSV line into Result<SampleRow, Error>.

In the loop, you put the rows into two vectors, input_data and label_data. You put the height and length into input_data and you put the category_id into label_data[7]. These two vectors are then converted to the Matrix type that rusty-machine models accept.

Normalizing the Training Data

Before you feed the data into the neural network model, there is a less-obvious step you have to take, which will significantly speed up the training and accuracy of the model. This step is called *normalization*. The goal of the normalization is to shift and scale the input data, so it has a

---

[7]You might notice that you convert the category_id from usize to f64. You might wonder why you don't just use f64 in the CSV format. That's because this is a categorical integer. If you use f64 in CSV, they'll become 0.0, 1.0, and so on, which doesn't look nice when you want to check the training/testing data with spreadsheet software.

mean of 0 and a standard deviation of 1. This is very helpful for models like a neural network because when you do gradient descent, a normalized dataset means the optimization process will not be dominated by one single dimension that has a much larger scale than the others. It also means that the cost function will have a smoother shape, which means the gradient descent process will be faster and smoother.

The normalization process involves two steps:

1. Calculate the mean of the dataset and subtract all the data points by the mean. This shifts the mean of the dataset to 0.

2. Calculate the standard deviation of the dataset and divide each data point by the standard deviation. This scales the dataset to a standard deviation of 1.

You must keep the mean and standard deviation of the *training* data at hand. Because when you normalize the *testing* data, you are going to use the mean and standard deviation from the *training* data. This is because all the parameters in the neural network model will be trained for the normalized training data. If the testing data has a different mean and standard deviation, the model's prediction might be off.

You don't need to write this part of the code yourself. rusty-machine contains a handy rusty_machine::data::transforms::Standardizer. The Standardizer implements the Transformer trait, which defines a shared interface for commonly-used data pre-processing transformations.

The Standardizer can be initialized with the new() function with two options: the desired mean and standard deviation. The normalization process you described requires a mean of 0 and a standard deviation of 1, but the Standardizer can scale the data to any other means and standard deviations. Once initialized, the Standardizer instance has two functions defined by the Transformer trait:

- fit(): Calculates the mean and standard deviation from the input data and stores it inside the Standardizer instance.

- transform(): Does the transformation on the provided data using the mean and standard deviation learned in the fit() step.

You can see the Standardizer in action in Listing 6-19.

Listing 6-19. Using the Standardizer for Normalization

```rust
fn main() -> Result<(), Box<dyn Error>>{
    // Loading the training_inputs

    let mut standardizer = Standardizer::new(0.0, 1.0);

    standardizer.fit(&training_inputs).unwrap();
    let normalized_training_inputs = standardizer
        .transform(training_inputs).unwrap();

    // Train the model with normalzied_training_inputs

    // Read the testing_inputs
    let normalized_test_cases = standardizer
        .transform(testing_inputs).unwrap();

    // Run the prediction with normalized_test_cases

    Ok(())
}
```

You first run Standardizer.fit() with the training data to learn its mean and standard deviation. Then you use this configuration to perform Standardizer.transform() on both the training data and testing data.

You then feed the model with the normalized data instead of the raw ones directly read from CSV files.

Training and Predicting

Finally, with all this effort reading, parsing, and normalizing data, you are ready to build the neural network model. The neural network model takes a little more configuration than the K-means, which only has one configuration: the *k*. For the neural network model, you have the option to set the following:

- The number of layers and the number of nodes per layer

- The criterion, including an activation function and a loss function

- The optimization algorithm

`rusty_machine::learning::nnet::NeuralNet` has a `::default()` function. If you look under the hood, it chooses the configurations as shown Listing 6-20.

Listing 6-20. Configuring the Neural Network Model

```
use rusty_machine::learning::nnet::{NeuralNet, BCECriterion};
use rusty_machine::learning::optim::grad_desc::StochasticGD;
use rusty_machine::learning::SupModel;

fn main() -> Result<(), Box<dyn Error>>{
    // Loading training data and pre-processing

    let layers = &[2, 2, 1]; // [1]
    let criterion = BCECriterion::default(); // [2]
    let gradient_descent = StochasticGD::new(0.1, 0.1, 20); // [3]
    let mut model = NeuralNet::new(layers, criterion,
                                   gradient_descent);
```

```
model.train(&normalized_training_inputs, &targets).unwrap();

// Testing

Ok(())
}
```

Let's break this down line-by-line. In [1], you define the layers as [2, 2, 1], which means a three-layer architecture. The first layer has two input neurons, the middle layer has two neurons, and the output layer has one neuron. By default, the NeuralNet chooses the binary cross-entropy criterion (BCECriterion)([2]), which uses the Sigmoid activation function and the cross-entropy error as the loss function. Finally, the Stochastic Gradient descent (StochasticGD) is chosen as the optimization algorithm in [3]. The Stochastic Gradient descent has three parameters:

- Momentum (default: 0.1)

- Learning rate[8] (default: 0.1)

- Number of iterations (default: 20)

All these parameters have some impact on how the neural network model performs. Since this is not a book on machine learning, I am not going to discuss how to tune them in detail, and you can stick to the defaults. A vital skill for a machine learning expert is to understand the mathematical meaning of these parameters and learn how to tune them to make the model accurate and robust.

You collect all these configurations (layers, criterion, and gradient descent algorithm) and pass them to NeuralNet::new() to create the model. The NeuralNet model implements the SupModel trait. SupModel also has the .train() and .predict() functions. The only difference

---

[8]Actually, the second argument is the square root of the raw learning rate.

between SupModel and UnSupModel is that SupModel's `.train()` function takes an extra `target` parameter, which contains the ground-truth labels:

```
pub trait SupModel<T, U> {
    fn train(&mut self, inputs: &T, targets: &U)
        -> LearningResult<()>;
    // ...
}

pub trait UnSupModel<T, U> {
    fn train(&mut self, inputs: &T) -> LearningResult<()>;
    // ...
}
```

Therefore, you train the model by calling the following:

```
model.train(&normalized_training_inputs, &targets).unwrap();
```

This step will usually take some time to run because the neural network is doing all the complicated mathematical computations and training the model. Once trained, it will store all the learned weights and other parameters inside itself, and you can use it to make predictions.

Making the Prediction

To check if the model is trained properly, you have 4,000 new data points from the `generate_data.rs` script. This example only passes the height and length to the trained neural network model. The neural network model will pass these inputs into the network and calculate all the signals all the way to the output node. Then the output node will give you a signal between 0 and 1. A 0 means the model believes that input is most likely a dog, and a 1 means it's a cat. You can compare this prediction with the generated answer and see if the model is correct or not.

You load the testing data from CSV and normalize it using the Standardizer you created during training. Then you can use model.predict() on it to get a list of predicted labels (see Listing 6-21).

Listing 6-21. Predicting the Testing Data

```
fn main() -> Result<(), Box<dyn Error>>{
    // Training the model

    // Testing
    let (testing_inputs, expected) =
        read_data_from_csv(options.testing_data_csv)
            .unwrap();

    // Normalize the testing data using the mean and variance
    // of the training data
    let normalized_test_cases =
        standardizer.transform(testing_inputs).unwrap();

    let res = model.predict(&normalized_test_cases).unwrap();
}
```

The res generated by model.predict() will be a list of labels 0 or 1, which is the result you are looking for. Notice that it only uses the height and length part of the testing data (i.e., testing_inputs). The actual label expected is not given to the neural network. Otherwise, it'll know the answer. If you compare res with expected, you'll see that almost all predictions are correct. This is not usually the case in real-life applications. The reason that it can achieve 100% accuracy is that the training and testing data are artificially generated to be easy for a neural network model, and it's free of noise. But this example shows you how to train a supervised model using rusty-machine.

Other Alternatives

As you can see in the examples of this chapter, machine learning is not just about training the model. There are many data-related operations before and after you train the model. These kinds of operations include:

- Reading and writing CSV or other structural data formats

- Pre-processing the data (e.g., normalization)

- Setting and loading model configurations and parameters

- Visualizing the data

It's not really practical to write all this code from scratch for every machine learning application. You need a strong ecosystem with many pre-built crates to help quickly and efficiently implement the learning part without worrying about fundamental tasks like linear algebra and data manipulation. Similar to other fields in Rust, there is a "Are We Learning Yet?" page[9] that tracks how the ecosystem is doing. As stated on the page, the machine learning landscape in Rust is "ripe for experimentation, but the ecosystem isn't very complete yet."

For the foundational mathematical crates, `nalgebra` and `ndarray` are starting to get wider adoption. They provide linear algebra and array/matrix operations similar to `ndarray` in Python. Many machine learning algorithms also rely on the field called high-performance computing (HPC), which harnesses the power of the hardware (CPU, GPU, etc.) and parallelism. There is much experimentation in this field, like `std::simd`, `RustCUDA` and `rayon`, just to name a few.

If you consider traditional machine learning ("traditional" in the sense that it's not deep learning), there is `rusty-machine`, `rustlearn`, and `Juice`. Rustlearn is very similar to `rusty-machine`, containing many traditional machine learning models. `Juice` is an attempt to revive the ambitious `leaf`

---

[9]`https://www.arewelearningyet.com/`

project, which was abandoned after the startup building it shut down. They all have implemented several commonly used traditional machine learning models, but the development seems to have slowed in recent years.

As for deep learning, there is no mature library built from scratch using Rust. So to tap into the field of deep learning, your best bet now is to use Rust bindings to mature libraries written in other languages. There are Rust bindings in the TVM project, which is an open-source deep learning compiler stack. There is also `tensorflow/rust` for TensorFlow and `tch-rs` for PyTorch, which are two mainstream deep learning frameworks.

Rust has excellent potential to enable high performance and safe machine learning applications. But there is much more work to get the ecosystem ready for production use.

CHAPTER 7

What Else Can You Do with Rust?

The End Is Just the Beginning

You've been on an exciting journey through the world of Rust. You've learned how to build a CLI, a GUI, a game, physical devices, and machine learning models. What next steps can you take? What other exciting applications can you build with Rust? This chapter briefly walks you through some other areas that aren't covered in depth in this book.

The Web

The World Wide Web (or *the web*) is probably one of the most influential areas in programming that has shaped the modern world. People have high hopes about Rust in this area. There are so many interesting topics about the web; they can fill a book of their own. In today's industry, web programmers fall into two categories: backend and frontend. *Backend engineers* are responsible for the server-side, while the *frontend developer* handles the client-side, usually the browser. People often forget that the browser and web crawlers, which consume the backend on behalf of the frontend, are also software.

© Shing Lyu 2020

S. Lyu, *Practical Rust Projects*, https://doi.org/10.1007/978-1-4842-5599-5_7

Backend

Rust has a great potential to be a backend language because it provides high performance, no garbage collection, and security. The Rust backend ecosystem might not be as mature as other languages like PHP, Ruby, Python, Go, or Node.js, but there are already some frameworks worth checking out. The "Are We Web Yet?" page[1] curates a list of various web-related crates. For a full web framework, you might want to check out Rocket[2], Gotham[3], or Actix-web[4].

One of the most common operations in a backend is database access. There are database drivers like `mysql`[5] and `postgres`[6]. If you don't like to write raw SQL queries, you can use an ORM (Object Relational Mapping) that maps your Rust object to database operations. Popular ORMs includes Diesel[7] and rustorm[8].

Most of these frameworks let you build a web server on top of a single physical machine. But managing and operating physical servers is an expensive, sometimes even painful, job. Unless you have the budget and staff to operate a data center, most people will go with a cloud provider. The level of service can range from a simple virtual private server, a hosted Docker container cluster, or even fully-managed serverless environments. Serverless computing like AWS (Amazon Web Service) Lambda allows you to run code without worrying about server provisioning. AWS Lambda gives you a way to run your Rust code in

---

[1]https://www.arewewebyet.org/
[2]https://crates.io/crates/rocket
[3]https://crates.io/crates/gotham
[4]https://crates.io/crates/actix-web
[5]https://crates.io/crates/mysql
[6]https://crates.io/crates/postgres
[7]https://crates.io/crates/diesel
[8]https://crates.io/crates/rustorm

a pay-as-you-go model. You only need to write the Rust function that handles the web request or does computational tasks; AWS takes care of the maintenance of physical servers, virtual machines, ... all the way to the Rust runtime environment. AWS started to experiment with Rust on Lambda[9]. AWS also provides many hosted services like DynamoDB (a NoSQL database), SQS (a message queue), and S3 (a file storage solution). You can access all of these services through the Rust SDK called rusoto[10].

Note   You might see the term "Async I/O[11]" a lot when browsing the backend crates and their documentation. I'll briefly explain why Async I/O is vital for the backend.

A web server usually has to serve a large number of requests simultaneously. These requests are network I/O-bound tasks that might take a long time. To prevent a request from blocking all the others to be served, you need to introduce concurrency. Rust's native way of doing concurrency is to create OS threads. Whenever a thread is waiting for a slow I/O operation, it can return control to the OS kernel. The kernel can then let other threads do their work, and swap back to the waiting thread when its I/O operation is done.

However, OS threads have a lot of overhead, and context-switching between them is computationally expensive. When you have thousands of requests to serve, spawning thousands of threads is simply too expensive and might overwhelm the OS. To solve this problem, you can try to run multiple tasks on one single OS thread. Whenever a task makes a slow I/O request, instead of synchronously waiting for it, it makes an asynchronous

---

[9]You can find the blog post on this topic at https://aws.amazon.com/blogs/opensource/rust-runtime-for-aws-lambda/

[10]https://crates.io/crates/rusoto

[11]I/O stands for input/output

call and gives control to other tasks on the same thread. Some kind of mechanism has to keep monitoring the I/O operation and continue to run the task after the I/O is ready.

The concept is easy, but it requires two new things: a new syntax and a runtime. The new syntax is Futures[12] and async-await. Futures provides a way to describe a pending task, and async-await gives you a way to say where the waiting happens. This syntax has been discussed for years and is finally available in stable Rust in the version 1.36.0 (Future) and 1.39.0 (async-await). There is a "Are We Async Yet?" page[13] that tracks this progress. The futures-rs[14] crate also provides extra traits and tooling around the bare-minimum std::future::Future.

To coordinate the execution of Futures, you also need a runtime. Since the design philosophy of Rust is to keep the core runtime as minimal as possible, an async runtime is not included[15]. The two most popular umbrella projects that provide a runtime are tokio[16] and async-std[17]. Since both projects started before the Future and async-await syntax were stabilized, there were many experimental implementations based on legacy syntax and crates. But with the new syntax in stable Rust now, they are all moving toward a more unified future.

---

[12]In JavaScript, this concept is called *promise.*

[13]https://areweasyncyet.rs/

[14]https://crates.io/crates/futures

[15]Before Rust 1.0, there was support for green-thread, which is another pattern for handling the "run multiple tasks on one thread" problem, but it was removed before 1.0.

[16]https://tokio.rs/

[17]https://async.rs/

Frontend

In today's frontend world, JavaScript has an absolute monopoly. Although JavaScript is easy to learn (but hard to master), its performance is not very satisfying. Unlike Rust, JavaScript uses garbage collection, which means there will be pauses in the execution. JavaScript engines also use methods like Just-in-time (JIT) compilation to speed up the execution, but this leads to unpredictable performances. Asm.js was created to address this problem. Asm.js is a subset of JavaScript that is easier to optimize. You can write in languages like C or C++ and compile them to asm.js. Because asm.js deliberately chose a small subset of JavaScript, it can run much faster and without garbage collection.

The lessons from asm.js eventually lead to the development of WebAssembly, sometimes abbreviated as WASM. WebAssembly is a standard for a binary code format that languages like C, C++, and Rust can compile to. The compiled program can then be run in a virtual machine inside the web browser[18], alongside JavaScript. It can provide high-performance applications in the web browser. WebAssembly is not intended to replace JavaScript, but to augment it. For example, you can rewrite the performance bottleneck in Rust and make it work together with the JavaScript around it.

The Rust official website has a dedicated page for WebAssembly: https://www.rust-lang.org/what/wasm. There is also a WASM working group[19] that is actively developing the WebAssembly ecosystem in Rust. They maintain an excellent tool called wasm-pack that is a one-stop-shop for building, testing, and publishing your Rust to WebAssembly projects. When a Rust project is compiled to WebAssembly and packaged by wasm-pack, it can be published to npm, the JavaScript package registry.

---

[18]WebAssembly can theoretically run in other host environments. However, most of the focus is on running in web browsers at the moment.

[19]https://rustwasm.github.io/

241

Under the hood, `wasm-pack` uses `wasm-bindgen`, the WASM/JavaScript binding generator. This crate can generate binding codes between Rust (compiled to WASM) and JavaScript so that you can pass data and functions between the two languages without much hassle.

They also provide two crates—`js-sys` and `web-sys`—to help you integrate your Rust code with JavaScript APIs. `Js-sys` contains Rust bindings for core JavaScript APIs, for example objects, functions, and arrays. But keep in mind that `js-sys` only contains JavaScript APIs that exist in all environments, including the browser and Node.js. The web APIs like the DOM (Document Object Model) and other things you'll find in your browser's global `window` object are exposed in the `web-sys` crate. With these tools and bindings, you can easily build Rust programs that can be compiled to WebAssembly and work seamlessly with JavaScript in any modern browser.

Web Browser and Crawler

When people discuss the web in terms of frontend and backend, they often omit what sits in between, the web browser. The reason people often omit it is because there are only a handful of browsers available on the market, so they are considered somewhat set in stone. You might protest that there are hundreds of browsers you can find on Wikipedia[20], but in fact, most modern[21] browsers are powered by three browser engines:

- Blink: Chromium, Google Chrome, Microsoft Edge, and Opera

---

[20]Wikipedia page titled "List of Web Browsers": `https://en.wikipedia.org/wiki/List of web browsers`

[21]Internet Explorer is powered by Trident, but Microsoft has stopped developing new versions of Internet Explorer and is encouraging users to switch to Microsoft Edge. See `https://www.microsoft.com/en-us/microsoft-365/windows/end-of-ie-support`.

- Gecko: Firefox

- WebKit: Safari

There is also a browser engine written in Rust from the ground up, called *Servo*[22]. Servo is one of the most significant projects written in Rust. The Servo project started in 2012, and it now has roughly 2.6 million lines of code (not all Rust, but still impressive). Servo started as a research project. But in 2017, the CSS engine it contains matured and merged into Gecko, the browser engine that powers Mozilla's Firefox. The rendering component of Servo, called WebRender, was integrated into Firefox later as well. So if you are using Firefox right now, you are also executing a big chunk of Rust code.

Servo has a significant impact on Rust itself. The two projects share some core developers, and the core contributors worked closely with each other because they were all started as research projects under Mozilla Research. Many of Servo's needs drive the development of new features in Rust, and Rust's design also heavily influenced how Servo is architectured. If you are interested in seeing Rust in large-scale projects, Servo is definitely a fun piece of work to dive into.

Browsers are for human beings. However, many programs also consume web pages. These programs are usually referred to as *web crawlers, scrapers,* or *spiders.* They "crawl" through web pages and extract information from them. A use case might be when you want to compare prices listed on different e-commerce websites, but these websites don't provide APIs. You can utilize a crawler to crawl through their web pages and extract the price information from the HTML. There are a few

---

[22]https://github.com/servo/servo

frameworks for building web crawlers, for example maman[23], spider[24], and url-crawler[25]. If you want more fine-grained control over the crawling and parsing process, you can use the reqwest[26] HTTP client library to download the HTML page, and use an HTML parsing/querying library to parse the page and extract data. Some popular HTML parsing/querying library include html5ever[27], scraper[28], and select[29].

Mobile

Chapter 3 talked about how to build a GUI for the desktop. But it didn't talk about how to build GUIs for mobile devices (i.e., apps). The most dominant mobile platforms are Google's Android and Apple's iOS. Android apps are written with Java or Kotlin, while iOS apps are written in Objective-C or Swift. Sadly, Rust can't be a drop-in replacement for these natively supported languages. But both Android and iOS have some mechanism for invoking (and being invoked by) C or C++ libraries. These mechanisms are crucial for performance-critical applications, which build the user interface in Java/Kotlin/Objective-C/Swift and offload the computation-intensive part to C/C++ libraries. Since you can compile Rust to a library that looks and feels like a C library, you can also use this mechanism to build an app that has business logic written in Rust.

---

[23]https://crates.io/crates/maman
[24]https://crates.io/crates/spider
[25]https://crates.io/crates/url-crawler
[26]https://crates.io/crates/reqwest
[27]https://crates.io/crates/html5ever
[28]https://crates.io/crates/scraper
[29]https://crates.io/crates/select

For Android, the process is as follows:[30]

1. Install the Android Studio (containing the Android SDK). This is the official development environment for Android apps.

2. Install the Android NDK (Native Development Kit). This toolkit allows you to compile Rust into a library that can work on Android and interact with Java/Kotlin. There is a `cargo ndk`[31] command you can install to simplify the compilation process.

3. Use `rustup` to install the Android targets; for example, `armv7-linux-androideabi`.

4. Build your Rust library project and compile it to a library file. You need to expose your Rust code to Java through the JNI (Java Native Interface). The `jni`[32] crate helps you with that process.

5. Import the Rust library into your Java/Kotlin Android app project and call the library inside your Java/Kotlin code.

The steps in iOS[33] are very similar:

1. Install Xcode, which is the official development environment for iOS apps.

---

[30]Mozilla published a post that guides you through the process step by step. See `https://mozilla.github.io/firefox-browser-architecture/experiments/2017-09-21-rust-on-android.html`

[31]`https://github.com/bbqsrc/cargo-ndk`

[32]`https://crates.io/crates/jni`

[33]Here is the Mozilla post on iOS: `https://mozilla.github.io/firefox-browser-architecture/experiments/2017-09-06-rust-on-ios.html`

2. Use `rustup` to install the iOS targets; for example, `armv7-apple-ios`.

3. Build your Rust library project and compile it to a library file. You also need to expose a C-style header file, so iOS can consume the Rust library as if it's a C library.

4. Import the Rust library into your Xcode and call the library inside your Objective-C/Swift code.

If you want to avoid building the same code twice, you might want to consider using Flutter. Flutter is a cross-platform UI toolkit developed by Google, and it will be the UI toolkit for Fuchsia, Google's upcoming OS. Currently, Flutter uses the Dart programming language for building the UI. Then it can run on both Android and iOS. Rust libraries can be packaged as Flutter plugins and be invoked from the Dart code, so you can build a Flutter frontend and a Rust library architecture similar to the Android and iOS ones you've seen before. The `flutter-rs`[34] project will help you integrate Rust with Flutter.

If you are looking for purely-Rust mobile applications, you can still build it the hard way on Android. You can use the `android-rs-glue`[35] project to package your Rust code into an APK file. You still need the Android SDK and NDK, but the `android-rs-glue` project provides a Docker image, which contains all the necessary setup and wiring to cross-compile your Rust code into an Android-compatible library. Then it creates a thin wrapper APK that invokes the main function in your Rust library immediately. Android-rs-glue also provides an `android_glue`[36] crate, which gives the Rust code access to JNI. This can be used to render to the

---

[34]https://github.com/flutter-rs/flutter-rs
[35]https://github.com/rust-windowing/android-rs-glue
[36]https://crates.io/crates/androidglue

screen and accept user inputs. But since this doesn't give you access to native UI widgets, you have to render everything inside the Rust code via OpenGL or Vulkan, similar to most of the full-screen games app you may find.

Note   The idea of compiling Rust into a shared library and using it inside other programming languages using their FFI (foreign function interface) mechanisms can be applied not only in the mobile realm. The Rust FFI Omnibus website[37] collects such examples for various programming languages:

- C
- Ruby
- Python
- Haskell
- Node.js
- C#
- Julia

It can also work the other way around. Rust can call libraries written in other languages like C. Reference the section "Using Extern Functions to Call External Code"[38] from the Rust book to learn more.

---

[37]http://jakegoulding.com/rust-ffi-omnibus/basics/

[38]https://doc.rust-lang.org/book/ch19-01-unsafe-rust.html#using-extern-functions-to-call-external-code

Operating Systems and Embedded Devices

As mentioned at the end of Chapter 5, there are many more things you can do at the hardware level than just show a blinking LED. There are simply too many hardware platforms and peripherals out there; writing bare-metal Rust programs for every one of them from scratch is almost impossible. Thankfully, there are some software abstractions already defined at various layers. At the bottom-most layer, there are peripheral access crates that contain register definitions and low-level details of the microcontrollers. On top of that, there is the embedded-hal layer. The -hal suffix stands for Hardware Abstraction Layer. The embedded-hal is a few traits that define a hardware-agnostic interface between a specific HAL implementation and drivers. Drivers can be written against the embedded-hal traits without worrying about hardware-specific details. This enables developers to build portable drivers, firmware, and applications on top of this abstraction layer. You can find many embedded-hal crates and their implementations by searching with the keywords embedded-hal or embedded-hal-impl on crates.io.

Building on top of embedded-hal are driver crates and board support crates. Drivers give you platform-agnostic support to a specific kind of device like sensors, modems, LCD controllers, etc. Board support crates give you support for a specific development board.

Many Rust developers also take on the challenge of building operating systems in Rust. One of the relatively mature ones is Redox OS[39] (see Figure 7-1), which is designed with the microkernel architecture. It already has a GUI and some useful applications running on it. There is also Tock[40], which targets IoT (Internet-of-Things) devices with low-memory and low-power constraints.

---

[39]https://www.redox-os.org/
[40]https://www.tockos.org

There are OSes for teaching purposes, like the intermezzOS[41] and Blog OS[42]. There are also a few less active ones that take a language-based approach, which means their focus is to build a minimal OS that can run a Rust program. This includes rustboot, later forked into RustOS, then further forked into QuiltOS. But most of them have not been actively developed since around 2017.

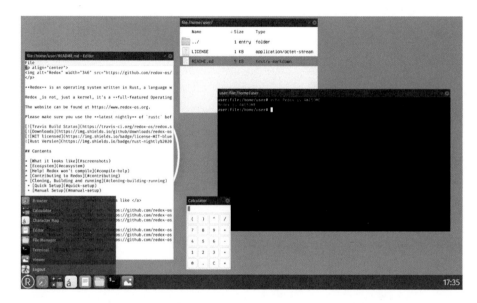

Figure 7-1. *Redox OS. Image retrieved from the Redox OS GitLab repository. MIT License*

Unlimited Possibilities of Rust

Besides the files you learned about in previous chapters and sections, there are many more applications of Rust. Here is a non-exhaustive list[43]:

---

[41]https://intermezzos.github.io/

[42]https://os.phil-opp.com/ It's named Blog OS because it was a series of blog articles by Philip Opperman on how to build an OS in Rust.

[43]This list in alphabetical order. The order does not indicate popularity or maturity.

- Blockchain and cryptocurrency: Facebook's Libra cryptocurrency is built with Rust

- Compression

- Cryptography and security: `ring`[44], `openssl`[45], `sodiumoxide`[46]

- Database implementations[47]

- Emulators: game consoles and other hardware

- Multimedia: images, audio, and video manipulation; rendering 2D/3D content

- Parser

- Science: mathematics, bio-informatics (e.g., Rust-Bio[48]), geo-information, physics, and chemistry simulation

Rust is a wonderful tool for building almost any kind of application. At this moment, some fields might not have a mature, production-ready Rust library and user base. However, with the support from the passionate and friendly community, you can expect to see many more applications of Rust, from mini-IoT sensors running on low-power microcontrollers, to cutting-edge AI running on massive supercomputers. Have you found anything you would like to build with Rust? Let's all work together to grow Rust and unleash its full potential!

---

[44]https://crates.io/crates/ring
[45]https://crates.io/crates/openssl
[46]https://crates.io/crates/sodiumoxide
[47]https://crates.io/categories/database-implementations
[48]https://rust-bio.github.io/

Index

A

Amazon Web Service (AWS)
    Lambda, 238
Amethyst, 88
    audio systems, 143
    creation, 90, 92
    Handle, 107
    keypresses, 110
    spritesheet, 105
Artificial intelligence (AI), 187
Artificial Neural Network (ANN),
    see Neural network
assets_dir parameter, 94

B

Background music, 142, 143, 153
Ball component, 117, 118
Ball struct, 119
Binary flags, 18, 19
Bounce sound
    effect, 147–149

C

Camera
    location, 100
    set up, 98

CharacterSelectionState
    parameter, 95
Clustering cat breeds, *see*
    K-means algorithm
Collision detection, 7, 129
Command-line interfaces (CLIs), 6, 9
    advantages of, 9
    binary project, 11, 12
    build and package
        binary distribution, 41, 42
        crates.io, 40, 41
        disadvantages, 39
        source installation, 39
    cat picture file
        catfile option, 22
        key points, 23
        main() function, 25
        OPTIONS, 24
        String.replace() function, 26
    color printing, 21, 22
    error handling
        Cargo.toml file, 28
        context() function, 29
        error message, 31
        exitfailure Crate, 30
        failure crate, 29, 31
        file path error, 28
        function signature, 28

Command-line interfaces
(CLIs) (*cont.*)
Pseudo-code, 27
unwrap()/expect() on
functions, 26
handling complex
arguments, 14–18
integration (*see* Integration
testing)
cowsay algorithm, 10, 11
piping command, 31–34
standard error (STDERR)
stream, 19–21
std::env::args, 14–16
toggles/switches, 18, 19
Comma-separated value
(CSV), 200–202
Components, 89

D

DenseVecStorage, 101
Dispatcher, 113
Dogs *vs.* cats detection, *see*
Neural networks

E

Empty screen, 97
Entities, 89, 95, 101, 107, 137, 140
Entity-component-system
(ECS), 6, 88
Euler integration, 123

F

Foreign function interface
(FFI), 4, 247

G, H

game_data parameter, 95
Game, features of, 88
General-purpose input/output
(GPIO) pins
BCM numbering, 162
Cargo.toml file, 163
input pin, 170
layout of, 161
output controlling
blinking implementation, 169
LED circuit diagram,
167–169
source code, 166–170
peripheral access library, 163
pin types, 162
working code, 179–183
Graphical user interfaces (GUIs),
6, 59
empty GTK window, 62
glade design
design tool, 68
glade layout XML, 70–75
gtk, 82–85
GtkBuilder, 75
layout.glade, 69
result of, 76

structure, 67
UI layout, 66
widget hierarchy, 69
XML file, 67
GTK+ and GIMP
Toolkit, 59
image displays
GtkBox, 65
GtkLabel, 66
text and text image, 64
text source code, 63
widget tree, 65
input and button clicks
ApplicationWindow
function, 78
builder.get_object()
function, 78
build_ui() function, 77, 81
callback, 79
event handlers, 77
Gtk-rs object, 81
structure of, 80
program screen, 45
TUI (*see* Text-based user
interface (TUI))
window creation, 60–63

I

initialize_audio() function, 146
initialize_camera() function, 99
initialize_players()
function, 103, 107

initialize_scoreboard()
function, 137
Integration testing
argument triggers, 38
assert_cmd, 35
Cargo.toml file, 35
predicates module, 37
shell script, 34
smoke test, 35
STDOUT, 37
unit test, 34

J

Just-in-time (JIT) compilation, 241

K

K-means algorithm, 193
classes, 214
clear-cut line diagram, 217, 218
clustering format, 213
clustering problem, 193
comma-separated value,
200–202
concept of, 193
CSV file, 214
file configurations, 202–207
graphical diagram, 194
helper functions, 212
main() function, 211, 212
output of, 217
STDIN, 213

K-means algorithm (*cont.*)
    steps of, 195
    text parameters, 216
    TOML configuration file, 203
    training data, 195–200
    training data visualization
        Cargo.toml file, 207
        CSV reading code, 208
        Gnuplot, 207
        minimal gnuplot, 208
        parameters, 210
        titles, legend and axes labels
            code, 209
    UnSupModel trait code, 211
    visualization script, 214

L

Light-emitting diode (LED), 163
    anode and cathode, 163, 164
    breadboard and jumper wires, 165
load_audio_track() function, 146
LoadingState parameter, 95
load_sprite_sheet() function, 107

M

Machine learning
    vs. artificial intelligence, 187
    model creation, 189
        British shorthair cat, 190
        classification problem, 191
        comma-separated values
            files, 191

Persian cat, 190
        Ragdoll cat, 190
    operations of, 234
Moving parts
    adding players, 100
    storage types, 101
Music player, 146
MyState parameter, 95

N

Neural network, 218
    diagram implementation, 220
    gradient descent, 220
    nodes, 219
    structure of, 219
    testing data
        binary code, 224
        CLI options, 225
        K-means data, 221
        prediction, 232, 233
    training data
        binary code, 224
        CLI options, 225
        code structure, 222
        configurations, 230
        CSV data code, 225, 227
        K-means data, 221–223
        normalization, 227–230
        prediction, 230–232
        Stochastic Gradient
            descent, 231
.next() function, 146
Normalization, 227–230

O

Object Relational
    Mapping (ORM), 238
on_start() function, 99, 137, 146

P, Q

Physical computing, 157
    low-level control, 155
    Raspberry Pi (*see* Raspberry Pi)
Piping commands
    features, 31
    STDIN, 33, 34
    STDOUT without color, 32
play_bounce() function, 151
Player location, 104
PlayerSystem, 113, 114
play_score() function, 151

R

Raspberry Pi
    components of, 158, 159
    cross-compilation, 157, 177–179
    features, 156
    GNU compiler collection, 178
    GPIO pins controlling
        layout of, 161–163
        output, 166–170
        working code, 179–183
    LED circuit, 163–166
    NOOBS installation, 160–162
    output and input circuits, 156

physical button operation
    circuit, 174
    debouncing code, 176
    diagram, 173
    GPIO input pins, 170
    internal pull-down
        resistor, 171
    internal pull-up resistor, 171
    types, 172
    voltage drop and toggle
        code, 174, 175
    Rust toolchain, 161
    window model, 157
Reinforced learning, 189
RenderUi plugin, 135
Resources function, 99
Role-playing game (RPG), 88
run() function, 113, 133
Rust
    Amethyst game engine, 6
    CLI, 6
    features, 1
    libraries/frameworks selection, 4
        maturity, 5
        popularity, 5
        Pure Rust, 4
    machine learning, 7
    Raspberry Pi development
        board, 7
    source code, 7
    two-dimensional interfaces, 6
    use of, 2–4
    Web (*see* World Wide Web (web))

Rust module, 110, 143
rusty-machine crate, 191, 192

S

ScoreText struct, 137, 140
Servo project, 243
Sound effects, 142
Spritesheet, 103, 105
   definition, 105
   loading, 106
src/catvolleyball.rs, 97
Standard error (STDERR)
     stream, 19–21
Standard output (STDOUT), 19–21
StructOpt, 14
   Cargo.toml file, 15
   clap library, 14
   default value and description, 17
   error message, 16
   help command, 16, 17
   single positional argument, 15
Supervised *vs.* unsupervised
     learning, 188, 189
SystemData, helper types, 113
SystemDesc implementation, 114
Systems, 89, 90

T

Text-based user interface (TUI), 6
   advantages, 43
   dialog, 51–53
   dialog box, 48–51
   empty cursive screen, 48
   input form, 44
   input_step(), 56
   keyboard inputs, 50, 51
   libraries, 46, 47
   multi-step form, 53–56
   program screen, 45
   skeleton code, 47
   TextView, 48
   user input, 56–59
time.delta_seconds() function, 116

U

UI system, 135
UiText entity, 139
Utility function, 130

V

Velocity Verlet integration, 124
Vulkan backend, 90, 92, 93

W, X, Y, Z

Window creation, 92, 94, 95, 97
Winner system, 132
   algorithm, 133, 134
.with_clear() function, 96
World Wide Web (web)
   abstraction layer, 248
   backend language, 238–240
   browser engines, 242–244
   categories, 237

frontend, 241–243
mobile, 244–247
non-exhaustive list, 249
operating systems and
    embedded devices,
    248–250

Redox OS, 249
unlimited
    possibilities, 249, 250
WebAssembly, 241
web crawlers, 244
WSAD keys, 88, 110

Made in United States
Orlando, FL
12 July 2022

19671308R00153